I dedicate this book to all British
Servicemen killed or wounded in
Afghanistan, heroes all

# THE MAN FROM THE PRU

## MEMORIES OF AN INSURANCE MAN

by

## Brian Holdich

By the same author

My Indian Journey
India Revisited
The 2001 New York City Marathon
Stanground Boy

Published in Great Britain Brian's Books (B. W. Holdich)
4, Elm Close, Market Deeping
Lincs.,. PE6 8JN


ISBN 978-0 9521017 4 1

# FOREWORD

For much of the 20th century the insurance man was part and parcel of life. Many of them became trusted and good friends to their customers and their visit was a great comfort to many people. They were the kind of people who could be relied upon to give impartial, sensible and above all else, reliable advice and help especially in a crisis. That is why the term "The Man from The Pru" became a well-known and well-loved catch phrase in people's psyche.

Brian Holdich was one such man and although he was made redundant a good while ago now, he is still much remembered for all the good advice and sound counsel he gave, as well as his pastoral care for his customers.

I am often asked, when I visit parishioners at a time of need, whether Brian still goes to church. When I answer in the affirmative they always ask me to remember them to him and say what a gentleman he is.

I have known Brian for all the nine years I have lived in Market Deeping as its Rector and he truly is a pleasure to know. Through this moving, witty and heartfelt memoir you will catch a glimpse of the man he is but also of the work of an insurance man in all its many coloured ways.

It will make you smile, laugh and bring a tear to your eye as well as bring back memories of a by-gone age. I commend it to you whole-heartedly. I am sure you will enjoy it!

Revd. Philip Brent
Rector of St Guthlac's Church
Market Deeping

# ACKNOWLEDGMENTS

First and foremost, I would like to express my sincere indebtedness to The Prudential for giving me permission to write this book. Certain resources were made available to me, notably any Prudential literature, leaflets, etc. which also includes the book "A sense of security - 150 years of Prudential" which gave me a minefield of information. I have also been allowed to use any of the company's photographs.

I am very much obliged to the Reverend Philip Brent, the Rector of the St Guthlac's Parish Church, Market Deeping, who kindly agreed to write the foreword to the book.

Not to be forgotten are those customers of mine who unknowingly helped in the production of this book. Fortunately my memories of them are as clear today as when I first made acquaintance with them all those years ago.

Thanks also to John Didlock for preparing the text for printing.

Finally, and by no means least, go my heartfelt thanks to my wife, Kathleen, for being a good Pru man's wife and who during my thirty years with the Pru took endless telephone messages, welcomed my customers when they called to see me at home and even helping with my book work. I couldn't have asked for a better secretary.

# CONTENTS

# INTRODUCTION

Being an Insurance Agent for close on thirty years with The Prudential, I have memories galore of knocking on thousands of doors and collecting the insurance premiums whilst chatting to anyone who was prepared to listen to me. I should, in all probability, have written about "The Man from the Pru" in 1992 when I was made redundant and my memories were still fresh. However, I was in the process of writing another book then so preference did not prevail. I never had the time, or indeed the inclination, for writing such a book, probably thinking that no-one would want to read it anyway.

So when I ceased to be employed by The Prudential, it was many years into retirement before I gradually came to the conclusion I should write this book - provided I was fit to partake on such a project and that I wouldn't slip into dementia half way through when all those memories would be lost forever. When I started on some research on those never to be forgotten days, I was pleasantly surprised that my memory was still good as I began to recollect such times. The more I probed into the subject the more I realised the wealth of material I had at my disposal.

This book, therefore, is in many ways a tribute to a lost profession and where the old style insurance man is virtually extinct, yet when I joined The Prudential in 1964 it was an institution known throughout the United Kingdom and the world. "The Man from the Pru" became a household name and I suppose in many ways the main participants of this book are my customers with whom I had such a good relationship. Many became good friends but they will remain anonymous as I wouldn't want to embarrass anyone. So this is my story of working as an insurance agent, more commonly known as an "Insurance Man", in the grass roots of a great company, where there will be fleeting diversions away from its subject but will remain a part of my story - a story of how the other half live and where hopefully there will be some funny moments. At times tinged with sadness, it is a story of how I visited thousands of homes as a representative of the Prudential where I had a grandstand view of many different and sometimes complex personalities. I believe my memories offer a fascinating insight into what it meant to be an insurance man which now seems consigned to history. I have tried to be objective throughout this book which I should have undoubtedly written many years ago, but surely better late than never at all.

On buying this book, if the reader thinks I am going to be critical of The Prudential then, sorry, you have the wrong book. (I don't intend to bite the hand that feeds me.) The Pru rescued me at a most uncertain time of my early life and I have always been proud to have worked for such a company.

# PRUDENTIAL WITH PRUDENCE

The Prudential was established in May 1848 in a room at 12 Hatton Garden, London as the Prudential Mutual Assurance Investment and Loan Association, by a group of Victorian gentlemen. It went on to become a national institution where virtually everyone in Great Britain had heard of its name and of "The Man from the Pru". It became an integral part of the commercial and social life of the nation for well over 160 years when the figure of Prudence was adopted as the symbol to be used on the company seal, which represents the value of business with the cardinal virtue of wisdom in action. The Prudential went on to become one of Britain's largest investors and a major provider of Life Assurance, Pensions and Financial Services. Its strength was built on industrial insurance for the working classes of that time where a new type of insurance was involved for the poor for a penny a week that in the event of a person's death the sum assured on the policy would pay for funeral expenses. This new system provided insurance on door to door collections by Prudential Agents to this market supported by sound investments and efficient administration. The success of this new policy encouraged the Prudential to introduce infantile insurance allowing parents to insure their children. This opened up a huge market and the volume of sales grew dramatically as that now famous policy of a penny a week had well and truly arrived.

Because of the amount of new business being done, the Prudential moved to Ludgate Hill, London in 1851, where the principle was established of prompt payments of claims which still exists today. In 1860 the Prudential acquires its main rival, the British Industry Life Assurance Company, which brings a large number of customers where the company now becomes the British Prudential Assurance Company. By this time the Prudential rapidly outgrows its headquarters at Ludgate Hill and in 1879 moves to its new chief office at Holborn Bars where the new building is opened to much acclaim and became a popular architectural landmark in the city of London. The Prudential was by now employing 10,000 agents across the country and the growth of the company was nothing short of miraculous as such a large operation was needed to keep pace with the increase in policies sold, with the now formed ordinary branch of the Prudential far outstripping its competitors, with the industrial branch dominating the field of industrial assurance. By 1914 the company was employing over 20,000 agents and had expanded its operations to every corner in Great Britain.

By the end of the First World War in 1918 the Prudential had paid out on 230,000 claims representing more than one third of British soldiers killed in that war. Prudential employers certainly served their country with distinction and of the 9,161 company staff who enlisted, 786 had been killed on active service. By 1919 the company moves into the field of general insurance offering insurance that ranged from fire and household to marine and aviation. In 1923 the Prudential establishes its first overseas life branch in India and business soon covers the whole of the sub-continent as the company gathers pace across the world by opening offices in Canada, Australia, New Zealand, South Africa and many other Commonwealth countries. On my two visits to America in recent years the name of Prudential was regularly seen and by 1924 Prudential shares are floated on the London Stock Exchange. It must be stated here though that the Prudential in America is an entirely different company to that in the UK.

At the start of the Second World War Chief Office staff are evacuated to Torquay for the fear of Holborn

Bars being bombed. By the end of the war the Prudential had paid out £5.5 million in claims on 110,000 deaths, comprised of British civilians killed in air raids. After the war an advertising campaign was launched emphasising the role of Prudential Agents in providing insurance to customers in their own homes. In 1949 "The Man from the Pru" advertising image first appeared in the UK being a familiar figure in his pin striped suit, brief case and bowler hat and was often the subject of music hall songs and jokes. As the years proceeded each new image dealt with changing times with a more informal look required. "The Man from the Pru" image did not just appear in the UK but internationally as well and became a global icon.

In 1967 Prudential's first ever television commercials are broadcast. The advertisements are shown in popular early evening slots and are seen by over 12 million people as business moves towards investment products, long term savings and retirement annuities as ordinary branch business becomes increasingly more popular. The following year unit trusts are launched and by the late 1970s the four traditional areas of Prudential expertise, the ordinary branch, the industrial branch, group pensions and overseas continued to be successful. Management of these diverse areas was strengthened by the establishment of a holding company called Prudential Corporation. Then in 1986 in the United States the Prudential acquires the Hugh Jackson National Life and in the same year Prudence is re-launched as a modern brand image of the Prudential. It was at this time that the Pru were employing nearly 30,000 agents.

Since my retirement the Prudential has come a long way from its humble beginnings in 1848 and its acquisition of Scottish Amicable and M & G Insurance in the late 1990s proves that. It has provided financial security for generations of families from industrial workers in Victorian Britain to twenty million customers worldwide. Famous for "The Man from the Pru" the company continues to maintain a sustained growth across the world. This very much applies in Asia where the Pru has become Asia's top European-based life insurer where the Prudential has forged partnerships with Asia's leading banks. This then was the company I joined in 1964 with its proud history and traditions. The Prudential's purpose has always been to promote the financial wellbeing of its customers and their families, with a particular focus on savings and security in retirement. What a remarkable success story the Prudential has experienced where for just a penny a week one could get life assurance at 12 Hatton Garden, London. From Prudence to Prudential it has been quite a journey.

# AN INSURANCE MAN'S POEM

Monday and Tuesday were the big industrial branch
collections of the week
I was well aware of this as I'd rise early in the morning
after a poor night's sleep.
Once a month on those days there would be a lot more
premiums collected
I'd start early by knocking on doors, say Good Morning
and hopefully respected.
Just the odd housewife could be grumpy if I started too
early in the morning
When on opening the door in her dressing gown she
might still be yawning.
On collecting premiums it was vitally important that I gave
the correct change
Otherwise if I didn't they might never forgive me and start
calling me names.
When in a house where there's business to be done you
may ask to sit down
Only don't do what I did once as the chair collapsed and
caused many a frown.
Be grateful on that bitterly cold morning you may be
asked to have a cup of tea
And later that morning if asked again, I'd say yes and rub
my hands with glee.
It's essential when in a house to create a really good
atmosphere in conversation
As it is so significant that your customers will like you with
no reservations.
If that nasty little dog is in the house it might well be
snapping at your heel
And on many occasions I'd be very tempted to kick it if
only to make it squeal.

It's important not to miss any bad payers because next time they won't pay double
These people are a persistent worry when in arrears, causing me lots of trouble.
Despite a really busy collecting day I might have to deal with a fire insurance claim
The poor woman would be worried sick but I'd quickly say she wasn't to blame.
Calling on homes I might see a new born baby in its pram and ask to have a peep
As it was the ideal time to mention a savings plan as the baby lay fast asleep.
If business couldn't be done during the day then make an appointment another time
Always keep the appointment as the client will feel let down which is a bad sign.
Sometimes when out collecting premiums I'd be knocking on doors in the pouring rain
So much rain would have fallen I'd feel as wet as a rat crawling from a drain.
Occasionally I'd be so busy I wouldn't have time to take the money to the bank
But I never did like too much money in the house as my spirits may have sank.
On arriving home at 8.30 pm my day wasn't finished as I had to balance the books
So if my figures were incorrect and didn't balance, I'd go to bed with a worried look.
At night time I'd put the money on top of the wardrobe and sleep with one eye open
Then I'd start thinking about being burgled with my sleep repeatedly broken.
But by looking back on the day then hopefully some appointments were made
So if new business was completed at a later date I felt I'd made the grade.

# OFFICIAL DUTIES OF AN INSURANCE AGENT

To conduct and service all Prudential business in a proper and constructive manner and to sell the company's policies and deal with any claims in a gentlemanly and cordial way.

# UNOFFICIAL DUTIES OF AN INSURANCE AGENT

Be prepared to put the kettle on for a cup of tea
Be prepared to listen to the local gossip
Be prepared to shop for those confined to the house
Be prepared to take the elderly to the Health Centre
Be prepared to report any child abuse or cruelty
Be prepared not to get involved in family arguments
Be prepared to attend many customers' funerals
Be prepared for someone disliking you intensely
Be prepared not to argue with hostile customers
Be prepared that people will use abusive language
Be prepared not to get involved with flirty women
Be prepared for a dog to try to bite lumps out of you
Be prepared to enter the filthiest of homes
Be prepared for sleepless nights when things go wrong
Be prepared if asked to be best man at a wedding
Be prepared not to argue over politics or religion
and
Be prepared to be on your best behaviour at all times

# FROM SELLING MEAT TO SELLING INSURANCE

When I started with The Prudential in February 1964 I admit to having no knowledge about insurance and because of this I joined The Pru with much uncertainty. I had strong reservations whether I was capable of being an insurance agent, at that time being not the most confident of people but part of me was determined to make a success as the options of what I wanted to do for the rest of my life were dwindling alarmingly. The responsibility of this not long married man were multiplying considerably. My wife Kathleen was expecting our first baby and only months previously we had bought our first house with a whopping great mortgage. I knew it was appropriate for me to find a job quickly and find a more settled occupation. I had tried other jobs in various parts of the country but I'd still been unable to find that certain employment I was searching for as I wanted more security, which would hopefully bring more stability to my life.

Previously to joining The Pru in the last five years I had completed two years' National Service as a soldier in Hong Kong and had finished my apprenticeship as an Electrical Fitter in Peterborough. Being the son of a butcher I did at least have some knowledge of the meat trade, which is what I decided to do next. So in next to no time I was being whisked off to Chester as a wholesale trainee meat salesman which meant calling on butchers shops in Cheshire and North Wales getting orders for large hinds of meat. What I didn't realise at that time, however, is that it was good preparation for what was to materialise when I joined The Prudential. The thrill of getting an order left a deep and lasting impression on me which I never forgot. Thus it was in that lovely old city of

Chester that I met my future wife, Kathleen, which proved to be one of the best decisions of my life when after eighteen months' courtship we were married.

After living in Chester for a year, the company I worked for moved me to Grimsby where for another year I continued to sell meat to butchers shops in North Lincolnshire, notably in Grimsby and Scunthorpe. With Kathleen then working in Grimsby we seemed reasonably settled, then out of the blue came an opportunity for me to join the family butchers business in Stanground, Peterborough. Unfortunately the move proved to be a disaster as the business wasn't big enough for three brothers to make a decent living, so at this time of my life I became increasingly disillusioned as to what I was going to do next.

Then my wife saw an advertisement in the local paper that an insurance agent was required by The Prudential. I had nothing to lose so I applied and within days Mr Bob Sergeant, a Section Manager with the Pru, came knocking on my door. He seemed unimpressed that I had no qualifications whatsoever to become an insurance man as he told me he would personally be training me. He told me the job was virtually mine although I would have to attend an interview at the District Manager's office at Stamford but that was just a mere formality. Although I had this fear of not being able to do the job, I was also optimistic that as "The Man from The Pru", maybe, just maybe, I might have found what I was searching for.

With Bob being my Section Manager he started by introducing me to all the customers I'd be calling on within my agency (agency means the area where I would be working), Bob taught me the collecting side of the industrial branch premiums (known as I.B.) where I'd be calling on my customers once a month or weekly. Plus the balancing of the books where I'd be subjected to an audit every six months because during that period I would have collected thousands of pounds. I was taught how to deal with the many complex claims where I would be involved with notably death claims, house insurance claims and motor claims. I'd be responsible for countless correspondence with receiving letters and answering them in the appropriate manner. Being an insurance man I'd be working from home so I converted one of our bedrooms into an office where, on average, I'd be spending one and a half days a week.

Most importantly, Bob spoke of the never to be forgotten subject of finding new prospects in order to write up new business. After a month I was sent on a two-week training course at Skegness which I found daunting but at other times stimulating. On arriving home I learned that Bob would be working elsewhere on his section as he had six other insurance agents to work with beside me and couldn't spend any more time with me. This news was all I needed as I was so dependent on him and how was I going to manage on my own. With Bob living fifteen miles away in Stamford, it's known that when one is in difficulties one either sinks or swims. Well I chose to swim and somehow kept afloat even though I thought I might drown, but survive I did and I believe it was the making of me.

At the start of my employment with The Pru I lived in Stanground, on the South side of Peterborough. It was a company requirement stated at my interview that I had to move house to Werrington, which was north of the city and where my agency was based. So in 1967 we moved from Stanground to Werrington and what a difference I found in moving with much less travelling in my car than before. It meant also I could spend more time on my agency with, hopefully, finding new customers to call on. More importantly, my customers would know where I lived which was so essential if they wanted to see me.

# A DISTINGUISHED LOOKING BREED

On first joining The Prudential I didn't realise that I would be joining the Stamford district which was regarded as one of the top districts in the whole of the F division. The F division comprised of district offices in the towns and cities in Lincolnshire and parts of the Midlands and spreading up to South Yorkshire. As the Prudential operated all over the country it meant there were other divisions the length and breadth of Great Britain where some districts would be employing as many as twenty insurance agents, along with office workers. Section managers, Life Inspectors who would all come under the control of a District Manager. It was strange that as my agency was in Peterborough that I should be attached to the District Office in the town of Stamford, not that it bothered me much as I quickly realised when I attended my first district meeting at Stamford I couldn't possibly have joined a more affluent district. It wasn't possible to have found a more distinguished looking breed of insurance agents in the whole of the F division.

My very first district meeting at Stamford was the opportunity for me to meet many of the field staff (being the outdoor staff who are dealing with the general public). These fellow insurance agents created quite an impression with me as they really were an eminent-looking lot. Being of smart appearance with loads of personality as one would expect "The Man from The Pru" to be. Most of them had worked for the company over twenty-five years and were men of vast experience in the insurance industry. I was the only one under the age of twenty six and very much the junior member. So because of that age gap I did feel slightly intimidated to be in their presence. Having said that, they really did make me extremely welcome which, of course, I appreciated because of their experience but I did wonder how I was going to compete with such successful people. At these district meetings I was inclined to say nothing and let them do the talking as my participation to the success of such a meeting was practically nil.

With the success of the Stamford District over many years, some of these insurance agents would have attended many of the company's star dinners which were held yearly to reward members of the field staff who had produced in some instances extraordinary amounts of new business. The stars, as they were known, had travelled from all over Great Britain and over a weekend they would be put up at a plush London hotel to be wined, dined and royally entertained amongst many congratulations from the management of The Pru. It would be an unforgettable occasion and I'm sure those Stamford agents would think how fortunate they were to be working in such a prosperous district. There were three RAF stations at Wittering, North Luffenham and Cottesmore where much new business had been obtained which generally kept the Stamford District in the ordinary branch (known as O.B.) in the top three of all new business done throughout the F Division. I have to state here that during my thirty years I was never invited to a star dinner-just one would have been special but it wasn't to be. In conclusion, I wasn't good enough.

It must not be forgotten that "The Man from The Pru" was a formidable character in the villages around Stamford all those years ago and would be much respected in the community where he lived. Becoming a village counsellor and perhaps serving on the local village Church Council. They might even be a school governor at the local school. It meant giving that something back to the village he might have lived in all his life. He might be a regular drinker at the village pub after he'd played his game of bowls or other activities he might well be involved in. His love for the community was such that he would embrace village life with all the fortitude he could muster and where he knew everyone. It wasn't too difficult to understand  why he was so successful as "The man from The Pru".

# UNCLE BOB - MY HERO

Bob Sergeant, being my Section Manager when I joined The Prudential, was a hero to me and not just because he had great faith in me which never wavered. Everything about the man stamped him a bit special and just occasionally he would tell me about his experiences as a Flight Lieutenant during the Second World War. His Squadron in the Royal Air Force would drop food parcels to British troops on the ground, who would be fighting the Japanese in the jungles of Burma. I think in many ways he was most fortunate to survive such dangerous missions because when the Japanese saw a British aircraft above, they would immediately try to shoot it down and often succeeded. It is a fact that if these airmen did survive a plane crash, they would be shown no mercy from the Japanese and quickly executed. Bob also mentioned eighteen-year-old British boys on having joined his Squadron and on their very first mission shot down and never seen again which he found quite distressing. I think Bob was one of the unsung heroes of the Second World War and like thousands of others should never be forgotten.

I've already mentioned that because of his work commitments in his section, I didn't see too much of him in those early days with The Pru but he would still try to be with me as much as he possibly could. So when Bob finally arrived at my home, I had mountains of problems to ask him about and although I'd been on a two-week training course, I still felt I had much to learn about insurance and at times I needed his help urgently. The great thing about him was that he had such a calming influence on me that within minutes of his arrival all problems were quickly solved. I always felt rejuvenated to be in his presence so when we ventured out on my agency looking for prospects to write up new business, he was as good a salesman as I ever encountered. Just watching him sell insurance was an unforgettable experience for me. He also had a certain style about him which I'm sure was a leftover from his R.A.F days. He would have been the ideal role model as the image of "The man from The Pru", with his trendy moustache, pin-striped suit and briefcase with only a bowler hat missing.

He was also a most generous man and to my two young children he was Uncle Bob and would often bring them sweets. Going back to when they were born, he delivered the biggest bouquets of flowers for Kathleen I'd ever seen. Then when my wife was very ill and in hospital, even more flowers would arrive. He also never forgot Christmas with even more presents with the best bottle of wine for me. He was my Section Manager for the first ten years of my career with The Prudential. I never forgot when I worked with an Admin Manager who did the very first six monthly audit on my collecting book, who told Bob that I wasn't going to make it as an insurance man because my book work wasn't good enough. Bob most emphatically disagreed with this man, telling him I was a slow learner but getting there. Bob Sergeant was not only my boss but a good friend and a gentleman too who really was a bit special as his war record proves.

# TWO STRANGE WOMEN IN MY BEDROOM

After a couple of weeks recovering from the birth of our daughter, Julie, in 1964 by Caesarean section, Kathleen was still in bed and being looked after by her sister at this difficult time. Her sister's two young daughters were also staying with us and one day when I was out of the house working on my agency the front door bell was rung. So Carol, aged 12, answered the door to be greeted by two smiling women. She immediately asked them to follow her up the stairs thinking they had called to see the new born baby. Kathleen then got one almighty shock when two women whom she had never set eyes on before entered her bedroom and as she was not well enough to get out of bed felt decidedly uncomfortable. The two women must have wondered why they were in this bedroom and didn't know my wife had only recently given birth to a baby who was fast asleep in a cot at the side of the bed.

Kathleen by this time had come to the conclusion that I must have told two of my Prudential customers to call and see the new baby. The two women, sensing the predicament they were in were becoming increasingly embarrassed with the situation. My wife then asked them "have you come to see the baby?" The two women shook their heads and said "No". Kathleen then asked "if you have not called to see the baby, why is it that two strange women are in my bedroom?" The women nervously replied they had called to see Mr Holdich, their insurance man, about a member of their family who had recently died. They also remarked that when the young girl opened the door to them, she obviously assumed we were friends who had called to see the baby. Kathleen then remarked "but surely it must have seemed strange to you both that you were going upstairs to see my husband in a bedroom?" At this the two women started to giggle and a more light-hearted atmosphere was established with much laughter.

By this time baby Julie had woken up and any misunderstanding was quickly forgotten as the two women gathered around the cot making a fuss of the new arrival. It just proved that a new born baby expands across many boundaries and all ended well. So whenever I saw those two women again, I would invariably ask them with a smile on my face "Have you been in my bedroom lately?"

# MISTAKEN IDENTITY

When out collecting the industrial branch premiums all on my own for the very first time I was understandably nervous. Being at that time green behind the ears, I was also short of confidence as at times I dreaded what awaited me as in reality I hadn't a clue as to what sort of reception I'd receive when the door was opened to me.

One mistaken identity I can clearly remember to this very day as one woman on answering my knock on her door didn't look at all pleased to see me and in a rather stern voice, before I even had time to introduce myself, said "You will find what you are looking for in the lounge in the cupboard under the stairs." So doing what I was told, I advanced through the kitchen into the lounge and there was the cupboard under the stairs. I opened the door and proceeded inside, being just a formality or so I thought, of finding the insured's premium receipt books, marking them and collecting the money enclosed in the books. But life's not always that easy, particularly for an insurance man calling on a house for the very first time.

It was extremely dark inside the cupboard and I couldn't find a switch to turn on a light. Rather than ask this quite stern-looking woman if there was a light, I started feeling in the dark for the books and money. On virtually turning everything upside down, I was unable to find what I was looking for. So after many minutes of desperately searching in the cupboard I was becoming increasingly frustrated at the ridiculous position I had found myself in. Then the woman, who had heard such movement coming from inside the cupboard, shouted out "What on earth are you doing in my cupboard?" I then sheepishly emerged from the cupboard looking very embarrassed and on rubbing my eyes on seeing daylight again, said to the woman "I'm sorry but I cannot find your insurance books anywhere in that cupboard". She then laughingly replied "Oh dear, I thought you were the gas man who had called to read the meter".

I must mention here that in all the years I worked for the Pru I've not only been taken for the gas man, but the electricity man, a debt collector, a bailiff, a policeman, a doctor and even a vicar. "The Man from The Pru" is therefore quite an all-rounder if he can be taken for all those different occupations when knocking on doors.

# UNFORGIVEN

I'm sure that 99% of the people I ever called on during my time with The Prudential, I got along with them very well indeed. As in life generally, there is the exception and I could, I suppose, adapt the attitude by saying "some you win and some you don't".

But one particular woman was as unsociable to me as she possibly could be which had a bad effect on me. This situation happened because my Section Manager in my early days with The Pru was forever informing me to beware of any bad payers on my debit. If they were out when I called during the day, I must call back and see them in the evening. One such woman went ballistic on seeing me one evening and in an explosive voice shouted "Don't you trust me. I'm not one of your bad payers. How dare you call back on me, do you understand?" I understood all right with the fault being entirely mine and if I'd checked my own collecting book properly I'd have found she was a good payer of premiums and never in arrears. I tried my best to apologize but that fell on deaf ears as this person was hardly a woman of a forgiving nature. So to have made that good impression on her I'd well and truly failed miserably. I also knew that any business going in that house had virtually gone as I'd be unforgiven for what I'd done.

This woman made me a nervous wreck as I'd get so worked up with myself when I had to collect the I.B. premiums once a month. When I did go knocking on her door I was full of apprehension as to how she would acknowledge me as I'd stammer a good morning in the hope she might speak to me. She either muttered something or ignored me with the atmosphere quite intolerable. I must admit she was by far the rudest woman it was ever my displeasure to call upon and for 10 long years, being very sensitive as I was in those days, her dislike of me was obvious. Then an opportunity came for me to move to another agency where, most importantly, I'd be better off financially. Now I'm not saying for one moment that the woman instigated the move for me but it was a huge relief that I'd never have to knock on her door again.

One last comment, when in my youth and during my National Service days in the Army, I did some boxing. Whatever punishment I may have taken in the boxing ring was nothing in comparison to the punishment which I experienced with that woman. She scared the living daylights out of me, she really did.

# LIFE ASSURANCE IN ACTION

Very early in my Prudential career I was to learn the real value of life assurance in action. This happened when with Bob Sergeant, my Section Manager, we had finally persuaded a young man of 19 to have a 25 year O.B. endowment policy where in the event of his death the sum assured would be £3,000.00. Bob, who never gave up on a prospect, was convinced that sooner or later he would get his man, so to speak. Sure enough the young man eventually relented and a policy issued much to the satisfaction of the parents who had also played their part in persuading their son that he ought to have some sort of a savings policy as a way of saving some of the money he was earning. The fear being that the son was spending his money far quicker than he ever earned it and for this reason alone why the son should take on some responsibility himself. Bob proved his point and that was never to give up on a prospect. Unfortunately, what we didn't know was that tragedy was about to strike in the most cruel of circumstances.

Six months later from the date of the policy the father informed me that his son wished to stop paying on his policy. He was in financial difficulties and just couldn't afford to pay the premium any more. The father had told me this on the Friday and I said to him I would come and see his son the following Monday evening. It was obviously my intention to try to persuade the son to keep paying on his policy because he would lose completely the six months' premiums he'd already paid, his policy being no surrender for another 18 months. As the boy lived with his parents, I did emphasise the importance of seeing him and to make him aware of the situation. The father said he would make sure his son would be at home to see me on that Monday evening. The position, however, was to alter most dramatically when on the Saturday evening the young man was killed whilst riding his motorbike, which meant the policy had become a death claim.

With the uncertainty of life we have to realise that such things do happen but the death of this young man shook me because I'd got to know him quite well. I had to understand, however, that deaths by accident or deaths by natural causes were very much a part of my job of being an insurance man and that I needed to get used to it.

In those early days to fill in a death claim form on someone where they used to live could be upsetting. With many members of the family present, with some in tears, and the death of this 19-year-old boy was a test of my integrity as to how I'd cope in such a situation where the family had lost a loved one. The parents were devastated and had asked me if the Prudential would meet the claim in full as only six months' premiums had been paid. I replied that I could see no reason why my company wouldn't pay the £3,000.00 assured on their son's life. First there had to be an inquest into the cause of the accident because another vehicle was involved and which dragged on for months before a date was given. At the inquest the Coroner decided the young man on his motorbike was the innocent party and no way was he responsible for the accident. Therefore, as it was an accidental death it meant the policy was double indemnity and that the £3,000.00 sum assured was subsequently increased to £6,000.00.

Just one final thought being that if the son had stopped paying his policy a month earlier, the policy would have lapsed and the young man would have no life assurance whatsoever and no money would have been paid out by the Prudential. Now I know nothing can ever compensate for the loss of a beloved son so when I presented a cheque of £6,000.00 to the parents, they couldn't comprehend why they should receive such an amount and they were completely overwhelmed being lost for words. I felt that the cheque may have softened the blow as the funeral and other bills hadn't been paid. I knew that at the very least the cheque would help the parents in that respect. The whole horrible incident spoke volumes for the great company I worked for, where in the neighbourhood in which the parents lived the good name of the Prudential was once more further enhanced because it really did show life assurance in action.

# SURRENDER OF POLICIES

Some mornings when out collecting the I.B. premiums I'd be greeted by a housewife on her doorstep with a policy in her hands. "Mr Holdich I want some money urgently to pay a large bill so could you tell me how much money I would receive if I were to surrender this policy?" as it is thrust into my hands. The policy was probably a ten or fifteen year endowment policy and on checking the date of the policy and providing it had been paid for two years, the policy could be surrendered. It was always difficult to give a true assessment of what the policy was worth after just two years. In answering her I would be as firm as I possibly could be by informing her she would lose out financially by not receiving back the amount of money she had paid on the policy. She was quite insistent that I still surrender her policy, even though she would lose out. "I've had no alternative. I'm desperate for some money so please surrender it for me," she said. Failing to persuade her otherwise, I would then proceed to get her signature for the surrender on the appropriate form and post it to The Prudential Claims Department and informing the woman she would receive a cheque in a few days.

The above is typical of what could happen with my customers on that first agency in Peterborough. They were often in critical need of some money to pay the bills. Some of my customers were genuinely hard up in those days so the surrendering of industrial policies was a regular occurrence. On this agency I had two large council estates and this was where most of these I.B. policies would be surrendered. Quite frequently some of my customers were always in arrears and one of the ways to square up the arrears was to surrender one of the life assured's policies and any cash back would make up the arrears. The agent was never allowed to suggest such a thing but those in arrears knew the system and asked for the surrender themselves. Any loss on my debit with the loss of policies was therefore top priority, as far as I was concerned, to re-insure the life assured, usually the husband or wife, with a further policy as quickly as possible. I would not only gain what I had lost but, more importantly, it was absolutely crucial to keep them insured being the head of the family. So if I was unable to re-insure them, particularly the husband, there would be even less life assurance on his life which would hardly be sufficient to pay for any funeral expenses on his death.

At times on that first agency I thought I was a sort of bank official by knocking on doors and collecting premiums, paying out the cash when they required a withdrawal of their money that would be held by The Prudential. For all the surrendering of policies my policy holders would be the first to agree that if it wasn't for their insurance man making his weekly or monthly collections, they just wouldn't be able to save any monies themselves.

I lost count of the number of times I was told that story going back over my thirty years. The great shame was that if those endowment policies had been allowed to complete their projected years, with the profits earned over those years at the maturity date the pay-out could have been substantial.

I must write here that the majority of my customers did let their policies run the years required as I wouldn't like to give the impression that my customers were forever surrendering their I.B. policies, which is not true. For those who did, however, it was a continuing dilemma on those two council house estates with the fear that if I didn't replace those policies surrendered with another one, I would be the loser. My recollections of those far away days of over forty years ago have never left me as I really did call on some desperately poor families. So when I knocked on their doors with a cheque or cash from the surrender of one of their policies, I would be met with gratefulness and relief on their behalf. Those smiles and, indeed, thanks more than made up for any loss I had suffered.

# CHASING THE BAD PAYERS

On that first agency to collect I.B. premiums was at times a nightmare and as I've previously written, some would always be in arrears. Those bad payers would also be in arrears with everyone else with whom they had business. Notably, the baker, the butcher, the grocer and the milkman would, like me, be knocking on doors and not getting an answer. As I've already mentioned, I did call on many council house tenants and I have to say that if I didn't catch them Friday evening, it was too late on Saturday morning as all the money would be gone. These people were only a very small minority of roughly 5% I called on but over the years I worked on that agency they gave me some headaches.

Even now decades later I can still remember those Friday evenings because Friday afternoon my bad payers had been paid. It was imperative, therefore, to see them and for about three hours on those Friday evenings I'd be chasing these people like a headless chicken all over my agency. I'd be driving my car like the clappers backwards and forwards from one such area to another. It was sheer lunacy as I sped from one bad payer to the next, a helter-skelter ride on wheels with no speed cameras everywhere like there are these days. The problem was that these people would expect me to call at precisely the time they would be at home but with Friday evenings being the big shopping evening of the week, it was virtually impossible to arrive at any specific time. I'd often miss them by just a few minutes as even I couldn't be in two places at the same time only to find no-one at home. Then I'd be joined by the traders who all wanted their money like me.

The main reason why it was so important to keep track of the people in arrears was that many of their I.B.

policies would be on the point of being lapsed as it was a company stipulation that I couldn't allow any of my customers to go over three months in arrears. So if that did occur, then all the policies in that home would be permanently excluded from my own collecting book. Although I hated the thought of losing one single customer that way, I never gave up on them because there was the possibility that the policies could be revived at a later date. Yes, those bad payers gave me enormous problems on Friday evenings but I was much younger then and I accepted the job for what it was and consoled myself that all occupations do not run smoothly all the time. What I found infuriating was when I knocked on a door knowing full well that people were in the house but refused to show themselves. It really was demoralising as I'd feel a complete fool that I was bothering with such people and would curse myself that I'd ever done business there in the first place.

I actually witnessed a bailiff at work when he was hammering on the front and rear doors and shouting through the letter-box in order to get the council house tenants out of the house. Evidently no rent had been paid for weeks and the people, whoever they were, had no intention of letting the bailiff into the house. By this time the police arrived and quickly battered the front door down, much to the amusement of the many onlookers in the street. The police then entered the house with ease which got me thinking "why didn't I think of that?"

# PEACHES AND CREAM

If collecting premiums on the doorstep was the bread and butter of an insurance man's job, the writing up of new business was very much the peaches and cream. Therefore, in his quest for finding new clients the insurance man would always be aware of any changes on his agency. This being why "the man from the Pru" was so successful over many years as he kept his nose to the ground. So much so that if new people had moved into a house just a couple of doors away from one of his customers, he would be likely to knock on that door and introduce himself and enquire whether he could be of some assistance to them as regard matters of insurance. Sometimes I'd strike lucky but the majority of times not so. It really was a challenge knocking on doors hoping that some business could be done.

I cannot say I enjoyed cold canvassing as at times one would get a rude answer. In this respect I've got the greatest of admiration for Jehovah Witnesses who go around housing estates in pairs knocking on doors. I do not necessarily agree with their views on their religion but believe me it takes real guts to go knocking on endless doors all day and because of that I admire them tremendously in their passion and beliefs. Can we begin to imagine the rude and impudent answers they would get from people opening their front doors to them? They must be very thick skinned and so dedicated with what they do.

Rather than cold canvassing, I tended to concentrate on the existing connection in those houses where there was already Prudential business on my agency. I was convinced there was a certain amount of potential there and providing I kept my eyes and ears open, then I would be able to strike at the appropriate time. This could be a newly married couple, the birth of a baby, when a 16-year-old leaves school to start work, when the father has been promoted and earning more and has he a pension? His wife now works part-time and now earning a good weekly wage, house insurance, car insurance are just a few of the instances where I could hopefully increase more business in the house. I was also very aware that another home insurance man from another company could have business in some of the homes I called on so at times I'd move fast otherwise I would lose the opportunity. It was quite satisfying to be there first, having won the contest, but with all the other home insurance agents I'd see on my patch the atmosphere between us was always friendly. If they did get there first and business was achieved, I just had to accept that this was what competition was all about.

It was part of an insurance agent's contract with the Pru that he was required to produce a certain amount of new business himself. So my priority was to sell as many policies as I could, irrespective of whether it was an industrial branch, ordinary branch or general branch. If I thought that an O.B. policy was a possibility, I would ask the District Life Inspector to call on a client in the hope that with his superior experience he would clinch a sale. There was the added incentive for all the company's agents to sell policies themselves, which would naturally increase their earnings significantly.

I also had to remember there was a yearly appraisal interview with the District Manager where he would have the appropriate files in front of him to see how much business I'd produced over the year myself. Fortunately my production of new policies over the years had been quite reasonable so I didn't have too many fears when these appraisal interviews came along. It has to be said, however, that any District Manager worth his salt would like more from his staff which was understandable. The real thrill of producing new sales on my own, whatever policy it might be, was always a pleasurable experience and definitely the peaches and cream of the job of being an insurance man.

# MY MOTIVATION - MY FAMILY

When working all those years as an insurance man people would sometimes say to me "I couldn't do your job knocking on doors all day and collecting a few pounds here and there and often getting soaked through in the process". I would look at them with some surprise because these same people would be stuck in a factory or behind an office desk and be bored out of their skins, while constantly watching the clock for when it was time to go home. In answer to that remark there wouldn't be too many jobs I'd exchange my own job with and as regards knocking on doors all day, that is not entirely correct. About two and a half days would be spent on collections with the rest of the week I'd be up to my neck in administration work where I'd literally spend hours in my office at home. In all honesty, I was never bored in my occupation. In fact, I'd say most of the time it was the opposite of boredom where at times it could be tremendously exciting and rewarding, particularly when new business was being done. I believe also that my personality was well suited for knocking on doors and exchanging pleasantries with my policy holders, many of whom I regarded as personal friends.

I believe that all occupations have disadvantages, even though one might have loved their work. One certainly had to be resilient working in all weathers in the winter. Like getting wet through and having to go home for a complete change of clothing was hardly Utopia. The winters of dark evenings were double the difficulty when collecting premiums as I'd make my way along many a passageway where I might knock over a dustbin or two while treading on a cat and knocking milk bottles flying. Then, suffering the indignity of falling into a thistle bush where prickly leaves would leave scratch marks on my body. The dustbin of years ago would be made of tin and when knocked over would make a hell of a clatter, causing the dog to bark and neighbours dogs also. So because of the darkness I might have disturbed the whole neighbourhood who would be watching TV. On finally making it to the back door, the resident on opening would remark "we knew you were in the vicinity because of all the noise you make".

On calling back to see a customer in the evenings, it was not always to collect premiums but to have a chat with the man of the house who during the day would be at work. The evenings were the ideal opportunity to have that conversation where, hopefully, new business could be done. During the day when I called it was usually the wife who would pay me. One such customer I was really taken back by what he said and, even now many years later, I can still remember our short conversation. I knew him to be a very odd-ball so I really had to find plenty of motivation to call on him. On his opening the front door I said "good evening" and out of courtesy I asked him if he was in good health. He replied "what the hell is it to do with you if I'm in good health or not so mind your own business" as he virtually pushed the door in my face. Now to get an uncivilised answer like that would test the nature of anyone, however placid one might think they are. I'd been told to ignore remarks, however rude and brutal they may be. So I'd learned to bite my tongue and not get involved in any slanging match, however impertinent or objectionable they might be. Maybe he'd had a row with his wife but his offensive reply was typical of the man so I didn't really expect him to be any different.

But acts of rudeness can be demoralising with one's confidence seriously shaken but I'd never be down for long as the next call I'd be welcomed with open arms and a cup of tea placed in front of me. This put everything in its proper perspective with the good far outweighing any bad. Usually by 8 pm it was time to go home to be in the happy surroundings of my family and when my two children were very young, just looking at them was all the motivation I ever needed in order to go and earn a good wage. On the evenings I would occasionally spend at home it made me feel rather guilty and I couldn't settle as I'd be thinking I should be working on my agency for my family as they were the real incentive for me to go out on the coldest of evenings. If The Prudential wanted more motivation from me then they were looking at the wrong person. Being with my family was all the motivation I ever needed as they were permanently my inspiration and it was for them I was working.

# A MATTER OF TRUST

The trust that was built over many years between Prudential policy holders and the company's agents was generally very good. Trust though is not just given to an individual, it has to be earned. So if the person is known for spreading many untruths, there can never be any real trust. A good relationship between two people, therefore, has to be built on honesty and confidence in each other before any friendship can be formed. So when out on my agency collecting premiums, it was entirely up to me to gain the customer's trust. The human element in the agent's occupation was an inseparable part of his success as an insurance man, which was hinged on being able to build and justify a certain amount of trust with his customers. Evidence proved that the agent was regarded not only as an insurance man but an advisor and confidant which went a long way to cementing that trust. The genuine relationship between the agent and his policy holders meant that the two parties got along together, otherwise it was doomed before it started. I believe it was a huge advantage to the Prudential and paramount to any success that was achieved as the insurance man was able to establish that trust, founded not only on unadulterated trust but honesty also as I eventually won my customers' trust over progression of time.

Trust though really is a two-way thing as occasionally in my job as an insurance man I would come across a situation where a husband and wife would be working during the day when I called to collect their IB premiums. Arrangements could sometimes be made with them that the premium receipt book, along with the money, could be left in the insured's garage in a hiding place known only to me. This arrangement over the years always worked extremely well providing the insured was in full agreement with the situation with trust being very much involved. Just the odd customer might well be prepared to leave their kitchen door key in their garage so that I would be able to unlock the kitchen door and enter the house, find the insurance books on the kitchen table and collect the money. I never felt really comfortable with this situation with allowing myself to enter someone else's house on my own, even though I had their permission to do so. I felt very intrusive, as if I was trespassing in some way that such a thing was allowed to happen because there really was a tremendous amount of trust involved. Say, for example (Heaven forbid) that something had gone missing from the house the day I let myself in, I could well have been regarded as a prime suspect. It doesn't really bear thinking about does it?

Calling at one such house one morning where I would normally get the kitchen key from the garage, the woman so happened to be at home and as I didn't see her too many times in a year, I mentioned that the arrangement of myself being allowed into her home there was a certain amount of trust involved. This woman immediately said to me "wherever I have lived I have always allowed the insurance man to collect the key from the garage and let himself into the house and if you can't trust a Prudential man in this world, then who can you trust?"

# A FLIRTATIOUS WOMAN

An insurance agent of whatever company he worked for must be aware of the pitfalls of the job by knocking on doors to be greeted by an attractive woman. I was very mindful of this when my wife and I, along with friends, visited a nightclub in Peterborough. I would be in my early thirties when a woman became a nuisance one evening as she joined our party even though she had not been asked. It was highly embarrassing not only for my wife but also the friends with us. Probably having drunk too much this woman was making a complete fool of herself and didn't seem to bother any discomfort she was causing. With her speech slurred and unsteady on her feet she was talking to me as if we were old friends, which we were not. How my wife tolerated this extremely rude and boorish woman, I'll never know but to her great credit said nothing as she would hardly relish a scene which could be even more embarrassing. As far as I was concerned the evening was ruined by this woman and I questioned myself how I'd managed to entangle myself with such a person. To her, however, I was her insurance man and she wasn't allowing me to forget that fact.

I believe that evening was a stark warning for me never to allow myself to get too close to any of the women customers I called upon. Talking on the doorstep to any woman meant a certain amount of friendship developing and I may have given this woman a mistaken impression by being over familiar with her. However, having a laugh and a joke with her once a month being part and parcel of my job from whomever I was collecting the monthly or weekly collections. So that evening at that nightclub she may have thought I was interested in her in view of the friendly conversations we had when she opened her door to me.

She couldn't have been more wrong as I've mentioned before in this book, my wife and two young children were everything to me and I had no intention of throwing all that away. I know we can all fall to temptation in this world even if one is happily married and it has to be said that an insurance man's job was often chatting up the opposite sex hoping, of course, there would be the opportunity of getting further business. In my case nothing else. Kathleen trusted me implicitly and I did her. I also knew that some of the homes I called on there were marriages not as stable as mine but for me I learned quickly that evening and the warning signs were there. Never to be forgotten also was that I was representing the great name of The Prudential where I was expected to behave in the appropriate manner towards my customers. So early in my career as "the man from the Pru" I learned not to get too familiar with the opposite sex, particularly one of a flirtatious nature. "So get behind me, Satan

# SHE WAS NEAR HYSTERICAL

How can one describe a certain woman customer without being disrespectful to her in any way because she was a very simple person indeed who could easily be manipulated by undesirable people who would prey on her vulnerability. This is what happened to a woman in her sixties by a man who took advantage of her in a most callous way. This woman made me promise that I would never divulge her name to anyone over the indignity she suffered from a so-called gentleman. So she will remain anonymous as I am not prepared to break that promise even though the woman has been deceased many years.

The incident took place over twenty years ago and the woman had lead a very lonely existence since her husband had died many years previously. She rarely left the flat she lived in and over a cup of tea there would be the usual chit-chat between us when calling to collect her I.B. insurance premiums every week. She was a reader of romantic novels where a couple would fall in love and live happily ever after. Hoping she might meet a gentleman in exactly the same way, she was a bit of a dreamer really but incredibly naive and saw the good side of every person she met, thus making her extremely vulnerable to the wrong doers of this world. She also lacked confidence to be involved with anything and had few friends, consequently I tried to encourage her to go out more and join things she might be interested in. Because of her inability to venture out of doors much, her chances of meeting that gentleman, as she put it, was virtually extinct. Her daughter and her grandchildren lived locally and were very much the centre of her life.

All at once it was very noticeable that she had started to spruce herself up somewhat by putting on make-up and making herself more presentable. She told me she intended to make the effort to go out more and was determined to change. If she was fortunate enough to meet that nice gentleman, however, no-one could possibly replace her husband. "All I want is friendship" she'd say.

Then one morning she greeted me with a huge smile on her face saying she had met a proper gentleman about her age and had asked if he could take her out sometime. Gradually over the next few weeks it emerged they were going out regularly and she told me the man had behaved himself impeccably. "A perfect gentleman with no hanky-panky" she told me. She really had become a changed personality and I'm sure she couldn't believe her luck as she was as happy as I'd ever seen her. I was really thrilled for her as she had seemingly met the ideal partner but at the same time I began wondering if this man was stringing her along somehow as she seemed as na'ive as she ever was and I feared that everything could go horribly wrong. If this gentleman, as she called him, was taking advantage of her in some way then this new found happiness would come crashing down around her.

What happened next is what I feared as this partnership came to an abrupt end in just two months.

One morning she opened her door to me in a flood of tears. Evidently this so-called gentleman had taken advantage of this so vulnerable woman by sleeping with her. She was near hysterical that she had allowed such a thing to happen and so ashamed of herself as she begged me not to tell her daughter. I quickly informed her I had no intention of telling her daughter as she sobbed uncontrollably. I did my best to console her in any way I could with much sympathy but she was a broken woman. Eventually I simply had to leave her as I'd got a busy day ahead of me but I felt so guilty about leaving her in her time of need with having few friends to talk such things over with being literally on her own. She could hardly consult her daughter as she would be the last person to confide in. This so-called gentleman had behaved quite disgracefully. All my friend ever wanted was friendship, no more no less. The guilt she felt over what had taken place in her flat meant that she never felt safe there anymore and was frightened that this man might come knocking on her door. Because of this insecurity it meant she had to move from her flat and she became more introvert than ever, so that so-called gentleman had a lot of answer for and a gentleman he was not.

# WHERE WAS HIS DEAD WIFE?

He was a man of few words and could I get him talking to me? No way. A very private person with whom I found it difficult to have any conversation. I used to see him once a year and that was to collect his G.B. house insurance renewal. One particular day I was determined to have some form of conversation with him regardless of what the subject might be. He was a real introvert who kept himself very much to himself so I knew it would be an achievement if I could get through to him. tt did cross my mind that he wouldn't talk to me because I was an insurance man and he feared I might talk to him about having some sort of a savings plan. When I called on him he was in his garden so the challenge was definitely on for me to get him talking as I began firing a few questions at him. Then he made a dramatic change in personality and I was totally unprepared for what he was about to tell me. I've never forgotten this incident and our conversation, which went something like this:

"Do you live on your own?" I asked him.

"Yes, my wife died a few years ago" he replied.

"Oh, I'm sorry about that, so you are a widower then" I said.

"Yes, I live here on my own but I'm not really on my own as I speak to my wife every day" he answered me.

Full of curiosity, I remarked "I'm sorry but I thought you were a widower".

"It's true my wife is dead but she's in the house right now" he says.

"What in your house right now?" I inquisitively asked him.

He immediately answered "Yes" and with a broad smile he asks me "Would you like to see her then?"

All of a sudden this man of few words was getting quite excited over his dead wife as a real personality change had come over him. As I was becoming increasingly suspicious by what he was telling me and I began to question who this man really was, what secrets were in his house and whereabouts was his dead wife? He could see I was hesitant about seeing his dead wife because I honestly didn't know what to expect.

"Please come into my house and I'll show you" he said and I rather reluctantly allowed myself to follow him into his house.

"She's in the lounge" he informs me.

By this time a strong distrust was flashing through my mind about this man. Was I being taken to see a preserved corpse as I didn't know what I was going to see.Apprehensively I followed him into a very dimly lit lounge, which gave out a ghoulish atmosphere that I might see a ghost of his wife? I peered somewhat suspiciously around the lounge.

"Look she's over there" as he points a finger very excitedly in the direction that he was looking. All I could see was a blank wall.

"I'm sorry but I can't see your wife anywhere" I told him. At this remark he started to laugh and then remarked.

"See that casket on the sideboard, my wife's ashes are in there".

The relief I got was enormous and I did breathe more easily once more. Every year when I called for his house insurance premium, he always took me into the lounge. Subsequently, I couldn't help but look at the casket on the sideboard filled with his wife's ashes.

When I got home from that first visit into his home, I gave my wife strict instructions that under no circumstances were my ashes to be kept in a casket on the sideboard. I know it is everyone's own choice as to where a loved one's ashes might be put but ashes on the sideboard is not for me.

# AN ANGELIC FACE

It was a regular Friday evening call to collect the I.B. premiums from a married couple who had five children. They were a nice enough couple to talk to but I have to say they were not the cleanest by any stretch of the imagination. The abominable smell once in the house was revolting and enough to knock me backwards. They lived in a tumbling old derelict house which was not good enough for any occupants. The house had been neglected dreadfully by the owner of the property and the husband told me their name was down for a council house and couldn't wait to move. He also told me the house was overrun with rats and as the couple were bad payers and forever in arrears with their premiums, it meant that I couldn't possibly leave them as I knew I wouldn't get double premiums the next time I saw them.

So on calling on a cold Friday evening in the winter, the effect it had on me was that I was stepping into a lion's den of rats. The husband had told me that the family were sitting in the lounge having their evening meal when they heard a noise from the sideboard and there was a rat looking at them. I have to admit I have no great fondness for rats and I did knock on that front door every Friday evening in a state of some trepidation of what was awaiting me.

As in similar circumstances, it was the children I felt so sorry for. They always looked in need of a good wash. I'm sure those five children, all under the age of twelve, would treat each day as the norm and wouldn't know any difference. The youngest child was only seven when I first called at that house. She was such a pretty child with an angelic face who deserved something better. It so happened that the youngest child was not only in the same primary classroom at school as my daughter Julie,

46

but sat next to her and they were best friends. When I heard of this situation I was in a difficult position as to what I could do to alleviate the problem. The predicament I found myself in was how to solve this plight and how could I tackle such a sensitive issue without offending anyone. The parents of this little girl were customers of mine and whenever I saw them they would often mention how well the two girls were progressing at school. It was a worrying time and I was in two minds how I should undertake such a delicate problem. Should I write a letter to the Head teacher at the school expressing my deep concern or should I take it further by making an appointment to see him and ask that my daughter be moved from where she sat or, preferably, be transferred to another classroom? People on reading this might accuse me of being standoffish by my attitude or, even worse, accuse me of discrimination against such a sweet little girl. This was not the issue here, however, as the over-riding dilemma was the health of my daughter who was sitting next to a girl at school whose house was infested with rats.

Rats are vermin and carry diseases which can affect human beings and only I had been in that house and seen the conditions that the little girl and her brothers and sisters were living under. Say, for example, if my seven year old daughter had caught an infection sitting next to that girl which was known to be caused by rats and died. I know her death would have fallen heavily on me for the rest of my life as the responsibility would have been entirely mine. I would have blamed myself for not acting in a more positive way when I had the opportunity to do something about it. In actual fact, I did nothing.

Finally, after much soul searching on my part I reluctantly came to the conclusion that I just couldn't possibly ask for my daughter to be moved for the simple reason I hadn't got the heart to do so. This meant living with the consequences of what might happen because whenever I ventured into the girl's home, she would often mention Julie's name and just to see the smile on her angelic face wouldn't have been fair on her for my daughter to be moved. As that sweet little girl who stole my heart couldn't for one moment help where she was born. I may have been wrong in the decision I took to leave my daughter in that classroom but, fortunately, everything turned out most satisfactorily, thank God, but it was a close call to sit back and do nothing.

# A MAN'S BEST FRIEND

When our children were youngsters they pressured Kathleen and myself for a family dog. We finally agreed and were prepared to pay £30 for a well-bred puppy. When one day I called on a man for his yearly house insurance renewal, it so happened he took in stray dogs. While waiting for the man to open his back door I noticed in his kennels the most whimpering little underfed dog I had ever seen. It was tied up and in a terrible state and the man on opening the door saw me looking at this dog and said if I wanted it I could have the dog for just £3 or it was going to be put down the following day. He also said how intelligent the dog was and being a Border collie it was a shame that no-one wanted the dog. Later that day I told my family and my two excitable children couldn't wait to see it so the four of us went to see the most piteous looking dog imaginable. The children fell in love with the dog straight away and pleaded with me to buy it. So I paid the man his £3 and took the dog home. The poor thing was in a filthy condition and the smell from her was intolerable. For a good week afterwards she was having a regular bath, which she hated, probably because she had never been washed before. In next to no time Slippy, as we called her, settled well into her new home.

When I was at home Slippy followed me everywhere and being really intelligent I am sure she knew everything I said to her. About a year later I went to India for three weeks and every evening she waited patiently behind the front door for me to come home from work. She became really miserable and even went off her food. Could it be that she had never forgotten the hell hole I had rescued her from?

When she was 13 years old she was put down which left us all in tears as she couldn't possibly get better. I still miss her years later. She was without doubt "A man's best friend" and I am convinced I would never have met her if I hadn't been working for the Pru.

# OH, WHAT A BEAUTIFUL MORNIN'

Monday mornings were not something I ever enthused over because on Sunday evenings my mind would be elsewhere as to what could happen the following day. I'd think who would be surrendering a policy, or would I be dealing with a motor claim or maybe a death claim or whatever claim I might have to resolve. I know it all seems rather silly, but Sunday nights would definitely be a poor night's sleep as I'd think of the I.B. collections on the Monday and would some of the bad payers whose arrears would be at a persistently high level be able to pay me was always cause for concern. With such negativity all sorts of thoughts would be in my head as I'd crawl out of bed on a Monday morning feeling like a zombie with not the slightest enthusiasm for the day ahead.

So it really was with mixed feelings of the unknown I'd get into my car to start my I.B. collections for the day. More often than not, those fears of what could happen would quickly evaporate. With the sun coming out and getting stronger it was promising to be a perfect day as I would invariably think how very fortunate I was to be as chirpy as a cock robin. Not for me to be imprisoned all day in a factory. I'd already tried that without the slightest chance of seeing the sun. So I'd often be singing or whistling the Rogers and Hammerstein musical classic "Oh, what a beautiful mornin'" and meaning every word of it.

My happiness was entirely genuine as I'd speak to every Tom, Dick or Harry out on the streets and on such a glorious day this "man from the Pru" would be chatting to his women customers. Young or old, large or small, and loving every moment. Being invited into a house for a cup of tea in the hope I might write up some business without pushing my luck too far because if I talked about a new policy too much I wouldn't have been invited into the house in the first place. Once in the house, I'd scan the newspapers for all the latest news from the Daily Mail to the Daily Mirror in the hope I'd get an unbiased opinion from some newspapers (some hope). The hospitality my customers were giving me made those Monday mornings even better and on arriving home for lunch I'd have that good to be alive feeling as all those negative thoughts which I'd experienced over the weekend had been abruptly dismissed for another Sunday evening. I felt completely invigorated, particularly if I'd made an appointment during that morning to see a client. "Oh, yes what a beautiful mornin' it had been with a bright golden haze on the meadow". On such occasions I had found what I'd been searching for and the only way I'd be leaving The Prudential would be if they sacked me.

# THE SADDEST DAY EVER

The saddest day ever when I was working for the Pru was when I heard that a fourteen year-old girl, whom I had watched grow up, had been murdered. Her parents were customers of mine whom I had called on for years and were a lovely couple. The young girl was blossoming into a really good-looking girl and I would call at her house every fortnight for the I.B. premiums at 3.30 pm on a Monday afternoon. Just as the girl arrived home from school, with both parents working, so the girl would pay me the premiums. This was the arrangement which worked well for years and the girl could be quite shy at times and just to get her talking I would enquire how she was progressing at school and gradually was opening up and speaking with more confidence each time I called. I'm sure no one could have envisaged what was about to happen when the young girl's body was discovered in her house having been murdered.

It really was the talk of the neighbourhood for months afterwards and people in the area were just that little bit worried naturally that a murderer was on the loose and needed to be caught as soon as humanly possible. Then it was learned that a young man had been arrested and charged with the girl's murder which was a relief for all concerned. At his trial the young man was found guilty and given life imprisonment. All through this turmoil I was still calling at the house and collecting premiums and I had a real insight of the anguish the family were suffering as the parents were obviously devastated over the loss of their beautiful daughter. The mother was inconsolable in her grief and I was at a loss for the appropriate words as to what I could say as all ordinary conversation didn't seem relevant in view of what had happened. I would try and put myself in that situation if one of my young children had been taken from me in similar circumstances as the bereavement of any fourteen year-old girl is always a terrible loss. To have a daughter taken in such a way by being murdered is too dreadful even to contemplate as I had seen the pain suffered by loved ones and I wouldn't wish anyone to suffer the pain the poor mother was enduring. I still have clear memories of that girl's murder which happened nearly forty years ago

# POLITICS AND RELIGION

An insurance man can be asked many times for his opinion on two of the most controversial of subjects going -politics and religion. Although I enjoy talking about these topics, I had to tread very carefully indeed as strong feelings can emerge and that old adage one should never argue over politics and religion is as true today as it ever was. So I was conscious on visiting customers on my agency that an Englishman's home is his castle. In the comfort of his very own surroundings that person can be quite scornful on such perplexing subjects. When a General Election was about to take place, I had to be discreet as the last thing I wanted was to fall out with my customers. I learned very quickly working for The Prudential what can happen if one gets involved in an argument while talking to clients on their doorsteps. One door was deliberately slammed in my face by an irate woman who used abusive language to me as she didn't agree with what I was saying. All I said was that a political party can be in government too long and that a change of government is not necessarily a bad thing, which I believe what democracy is about as a political party can become stale and disorientated. I learned from that incident to choose my words more carefully as more discretion and impartiality was required. If a discussion got heated in the future, I had to bite my tongue when a customer said something I didn't agree with.

At election time it was not always known how some of my customers would vote as for some it was a private thing where others were more vocal and wouldn't hold back in any way as to their political allegiance. What was interesting was that council house tenants would not always vote Labour which one would think was a Labour stronghold, where in some of the large private houses one thought of those house owners voting Conservative but voted Labour. Margaret Thatcher was always a contentious figure and people had varying views on such a high profile Prime Minister and was often the central figure of any conversation. There were no half measures with her as my customers either loved or loathed the lady. It was either a case of daggers drawn against her or their eyes would light up with glee at the very mention of her name. The 1984 coal miners' strike really was a controversial issue and was a good debating issue with my customers. With Thatcher in the thick of it and not giving an inch to Arthur Scargill, the miners' leader, I did my best to remain impartial. I often wondered how those Prudential agents were coping at that time with the areas affected in Yorkshire. I felt certain sympathy for them as the miners' strike proceeded on and how could the miners afford their insurance premiums whilst not working. I'm sure for everyone affected it was a difficult time with much relief in some areas when it was over and people could get back to something like normality.

"Mister insurance man," which she often addressed me as "you go to church don't you, so please tell me why God has been so unkind to me," she wanted to know. Now who could possibly answer a question of such significance as that? It left me rather confused while searching for the appropriate words in order to pacify her. She knew I was a regular attender at my local parish church and she seemed to be pleading with me to give her an explanation. She had been a Prudential policy holder virtually all her life and one particular morning she was quite distressed as some members of her family in a short space of time had died. "Why me?" she asked "If there is a God why is he treating me this way?" "I've had a hard life having left school at fourteen to work on the land and never owed anyone anything, raised a large family and nursed my husband for years when he was ill and I feel I don't deserve what is happening to me at my time of life. So please, if there is a God, why is he treating me this way" she wanted to know. She had assumed that because I went to church I would be able to answer her questions. I couldn't give her any clear inclination other than to say that God moves in mysterious ways and that He is always there for us if we need him He will listen to us when we pray to Him. I'm afraid that in answering her I failed her most convincingly. I was not a priest but an insurance man. I was asked many times over the years "why does God allow earthquakes and mass flooding in the third world with thousands of lives lost"? At times I felt so ill-equipped to answer such questions but I know I have great faith in Him and He's always looked after me and my family and once He answered my prayers along with a plane load of passengers when we needed him.

"This is the captain speaking," said the voice over the Tannoy when with my wife, our daughter, son-in-law and two of our grandchildren went on a week's holiday to Minorca. We thought the flight had gone well when the captain spoke those words. He informed the passengers that although we were just half an hour off Minorca, he had no alternative but to return to the UK as one of the engines had failed. He reported that Minorca airport didn't have the necessary equipment to repair the engine which meant flying back to Luton airport. Every twenty minutes the captain assured the passengers everything was going well and if the plane was experiencing difficulties he would put down at Paris airport which had been informed. I realised then that the captain would only tell his passengers so much as he would require everyone on the flight to remain as calm as possible.

It was nearing Luton airport that the captain in no uncertain manner told his passengers to prepare for an emergency landing. This was a shock and I'm sure all on board realised the seriousness of the situation. The flight was full of holiday makers with scores of children and some babies who by this time were noisy and restless with what had become a long flight. This then was the position as the aircraft started to descend into Luton airport. The captain had also mentioned not to be alarmed as we touch down as the fire engines would be rushing towards the plane, which is the normal procedure in an emergency. I had one final look at my family and the passengers and thought surely all those children are not going to die. I found myself saying The Lord's Prayer as I'm sure prayers were being said all over that aircraft as I crouched down in my seat with safety belt on, head forward bowed towards my legs and waited for the inevitable, whatever it might be. My last recollection was the quietness inside the plane with not the slightest noise to be heard. So it was that the wheels of the aircraft hit the runway with an almighty bump and looking out of those little passenger windows fire engines were rushing out to greet us. When the aircraft finally stopped rapturous applause broke out which must have gone on for a minute. The relief and sheer joy from the passengers said it all on their faces. So did God play a part in the survival of everyone on board? Well, I believe He did and my prayers and those of many others that day were surely answered.

# TIRESOME AT LEAST

Occasionally, I would receive a transfer of an I.B. insurance policy from a Prudential agent where one of his customers had moved on to my agency. On finding the address, I would then introduce myself hoping there might be the opportunity of further business. On knocking on one such front door I was invited into the house and the lounge, and in order to keep the conversation going I asked whose photograph it was of the smiling teenage boy on the sideboard. I couldn't have made a more favourable comment as the woman's face lit up in absolute joy as she couldn't have asked for more from her new insurance man.

I didn't realise though that from then onwards I'd be regularly subjected to so much lavish praise on how well her son was progressing at university. Try as I did on my monthly call by mentioning more serious incidents going on in the world, she wouldn't budge in her stubborness to stay on her favourite subject. So when she finally paid her premiums I'd start by backtracking to the front door in my haste to leave, but even then she would follow me singing the praises of her son. Once she got to the front door before I did and blocked my way of escape, and for a few seconds I visualised being held captive against my will. I couldn't even begin to comprehend why this woman should act this way, as it was a test of my composure that under the circumstances I should remain with a calm and cool head. I know we can all be proud of our children but to dominate all conversation like this doting mother did over her son, was tiresome to say the least.

# I'M NOT DEAD YET

Every three months I would call on a lady who was in her eighties. We always engaged in good conversation with each other and she certainly had a mind of her own. Having lost her husband years ago she was a very independent person and even at her age was nobody's fool. She could argue with the best of them and that included her Prudential man. In conversation with her it was usually light-hearted banter between us and she really was a delight to call on. In view of her age she kept in good health and if she was ill at any time, a daughter only lived just round the corner.

One particular morning on having rung the front door bell, a middle-aged woman whom I'd never met opened the door to me. This proved to be the daughter and without a moment's hesitation said "would you follow me please". I didn't know that her Mother was ill and evidently the doctor was expected at any time and the daughter automatically assumed I was the doctor who had called to see her poorly Mother. Doing what I was told, I followed the daughter. I must admit at this stage I wasn't sure what was going on and instead of being taken into the kitchen where the insurance books and money would be, I found myself being taken into a bedroom. Guess who was sitting upright in bed with a flimsy nightgown on and looking not at all well whilst waiting to see the doctor? As a way of introduction, the daughter then proceeded to say "Mother, I've brought the doctor to see you." At that precise moment I entered the bedroom with my large collecting book under my arm. The poor dear lady nearly had a fit on seeing me of all people and tried to cover herself up a little bit and in exasperation really let fly "That's not the doctor, that's the so and so insurance man. Get him out of here and I'm not dead yet". By this time I was beginning to feel rather uncomfortable as I made a hasty retreat from that bedroom.

Evidently the unexpected shock of seeing me that morning had no premeditated effect on the lady but I have to admit to being quite embarrassed by the incident. Even today I can still visualise the astonished look on her face when I was introduced as the doctor.

Moments like that continue to be increasingly funny and even now many years later still brings a smile to my face. The lady incidentally made an excellent recovery from her illness and lived for many years afterwards. When she was better we always joked about my walking into her bedroom to see her in her flimsy nightgown sitting up in bed waiting to see her insurance man of all people. So I told her "please tell your daughter that if you are taken ill again she must send for 'the man from the Pru', your friendly insurance man who looks like a doctor."

# AN ABUSED WOMAN

Perhaps to be an insurance man counselling should be required as I came across many instances over the years where my customers just wanted someone to talk to and that someone was often me. I mention this because many of my policyholders would lead a very lonely existence and wouldn't come across too many people to talk to in a week. I'm not necessarily talking about the elderly who are very much confined to their home but customers of all ages had taken me into their confidence and poured out their problems to me. Being a regular call, it seemed convenient to them that I did have a sympathetic ear as I would listen to their problems. Often it would be over some advice they were seeking but I had to remind myself repeatedly that I was employed by The Prudential and not to get involved with other people's worries. I really valued the friendship of my customers so I would help in any way possible as it really was a question of finding that balance of helping but not going overboard with that help. After all was said and done, I was an insurance man and not a counsellor. One such dilemma, however, was way beyond the duties of this insurance man and worried me continually when one woman told me she was being sexually abused by her husband.

Once a week I called to see this woman who would be in her early sixties and her husband who was about the same age. The woman was usually the payer of the I.B. premiums and there were times when her policies were dangerously near to being lapsed. In other words, forever in arrears which often meant calling back in the evening to see her husband in the hope that I could get some money from him. Now I could see the relationship with his wife wasn't good and I always had the feeling he deliberately kept his wife short of money being a sort of punishment if you like. I did find him a rather strange individual and whenever I saw him I felt uncomfortable in his presence. On seeing his wife on her own in the morning, she was often close to tears so because of this I did have some difficulty in having a normal conversation. At the back of my mind, however, something just didn't seem right as some days she could be quite talkative while other days just too upset to talk. Gradually we became more friendly and I did have a feeling that something was bothering her. Then one morning she broke down completely sobbing so much that I had to ask her what was the matter. "Mr Holdich my husband demands sex with me every night and I just can't take any more. I shouldn't be telling you this but I've just got to tell someone"

So how was I to act having been told by this pitiful woman that her husband was abusing her. The woman mentioned other things which I am not prepared to mention here and obviously my sympathies were very much with her. But why was she telling me this as I felt hopelessly inadequate to give her some answers and if it was a cry for help how did she expect me to respond? Did she expect me to confront her husband about this abuse which I wasn't prepared to do? How could I come between a husband and his wife? I felt for this poor wreck of a woman and nothing but contempt for this brute of a husband. All this happened many years ago but I can still visualise the look of fear in that woman's eyes. What was also very worrying was that in that house was an eight-year-old girl who was the woman's own granddaughter who permanently lived at this address. Now I know it's one thing for a man to sexually abuse his wife with me being in the awkward position of not being able to help the woman but if I'd had the slightest suspicion that the man was abusing that little girl, I would undoubtedly have reported him to the Police. However, she seemed a normal fun loving little girl who was very close to her grandmother who seemed very protective of her. Who knows what goes on behind closed doors and I always sincerely hoped that the girl was not affected in any way but I have to admit I was never absolutely sure.

# YOUNG AT HEART

I would have done anything, within reason of course, to have helped any of my customers in every possible way but even I couldn't contemplate that because of a good relationship with two elderly customers both well in their seventies, that by my introducing them to each other a romance developed at such speed that within a few weeks they would be married with me being asked to be Best Man. I can only describe them as young at heart and I am reminded of that hit song of years ago sung by Frank Sinatra which begins "Fairy tales can come true, it can happen to you, if you're young at heart". Well these two golden oldies were living the fairy tale proving that romance will never die.

I shall refer to them as Jack and Jill as both their spouses had died a few years ago and had grown-up children and grandchildren. They both lived on my agency in flats within a quarter of a mile of each other but had never met. Jill seemed to have a busy life being a good mixer with people and her children lived locally whom she saw quite often. Jack, a Norfolk man, had moved to Peterborough with his job leaving his grown-up children in Norfolk. When his wife died, he became a very lonely man and on my monthly I.B. collections he was eager to have a long conversation with me if only to pass the time of day as I'd often see him riding his bicycle to escape the loneliness of being in his house all day.

Then one day a dramatic change came over him when I introduced him to Jill when all three of us just happened to be in the same place at the same time. Jack's face lit up and I could see he was really smitten with Jill so as they seemed to have eyes only for each other, I decided to make myself scarce and left them in deep conversation. So well were they getting along with each other it was as though they had known each other all their lives.

On seeing Jill the following week, she admitted what a nice man Jack was but was slightly dubious of his persistent telephone calls to her and had asked if he could take her out. She informed me she would not be rushed into any sort of commitment to him as I could see she was worried how this friendship could develop. A few days later I saw Jack on his bike and full of excitement tells me "Brian, Jill's such a lovely woman and I can't get her out of my mind. I feel eighteen again and I love her and want to marry her". I could see he'd got it bad and there was no stopping him. But I remember telling him not to rush into anything as important as marriage. Here again I felt by giving him some advice I was a counsellor again, only this time a marriage counsellor. Not for the first time did I question myself in getting involved. Things then took one almighty leap forward when on seeing Jill to collect her I.B. insurance collections, she informed me that she and Jack were getting married by saying "as you brought us together Brian, it would be most appropriate if you would be Best Man". I must admit that I was rather shocked with the news and Jack's pursuit of Jill had obviously paid off. The way Jill had said I'd brought them together, how could I possibly refuse being Best Man?

At the wedding ceremony just four people were in attendance, being the bride and groom, a witness and me the Best Man. Jack and Jill had barely known each other two months and at the local pub we drank to a long and happy marriage. It did cross my mind that day that it was rather sad that none of the children on both sides of the family had made an appearance at the wedding. It was soon after the wedding that I was in the process of changing my agency for one at Market Deeping and once I'd moved house I lost all contact with Jack and Jill.

I'm afraid there was a sad end to this story, however, because about eighteen months after the wedding Jill was knocked down by a motor vehicle while crossing a road in Peterborough and killed. If anyone was going to die first, I had assumed it would be Jack for he told me once he hadn't long to live. The uncertainty of life proved me wrong with Jill being killed in a most tragic way Jack, I am sure, would have been devastated over his loss and I do so sincerely hope those eighteen months of married life brought them much happiness. I have to write that I didn't know of Jill's death until many years later when a relative told me. If only I'd known this at the time, at the very least I would have attended Jill's funeral.

# STEPPING OVER THE DEAD

A woman had been in contact with me to inform me that a distant relative of hers had died. Unfortunately, she had been unable to find a death certificate of the deceased having made enquiries at the Registry Office which had no knowledge of such a death. The woman had found a battered old Prudential policy and wanted to stake a claim on the policy. Evidently the life assured had been dead many years and the woman was the only living relative of the deceased. The policy was one of the original penny-a-week policies which by the date of the policy, was over ninety years old. There was no premium receipt book which would have given the necessary evidence when the last premium was paid so I had no idea what the policy was worth. The woman had also told me the evidence of the deceased death was likely to be found in a Peterborough cemetery because that is where she believed he would be buried. Instinctively I knew this would be a complicated death claim and what would be the Prudential's attitude as I curiously waited the reply to the letter I'd written to the Death Claims Department. But even I didn't realise I would be ordered by my company to check for the deceased's name on the gravestones in a most derelict cemetery that hadn't been used for years. Talk about stepping over the dead. Yes I did, dozens of them.

That day in a deserted cemetery was a real eye opener to see how such a large cemetery had been so dreadfully neglected. I'm equally sure that other old cemeteries throughout Great Britain are all in the same dilapidated state. It had been abandoned many years previously to rot and decay with some areas too dangerous even to walk upon. Some of the gravestones had been savagely knocked about and smashed to pieces by vandalism. While there I did wonder how such depraved individuals could resort to such violence and destruction of what would have been really beautiful gravestones many years ago. Treading on slippery surfaces in the depths of winter didn't help either, making it in some areas unsteady on the feet. So unsafe was the ground around the gravestones that at times I felt I might be swallowed up and plunged into a grave. In some instances I'd actually stand on the grave in a crouched position doing my best to try and read the faded names on the gravestones. Most of these gravestones had been there well over a hundred years and some over two hundred and fifty years. On some of the really old gravestones it was virtually impossible to read any names as they had faded away completely. The extreme loneliness I experienced was very real indeed to be in such a spooky atmosphere in my search to find a certain name.

For the record, I never did find the grave I was looking for having spent several hours there. The Prudential did eventually pay the claim having come to the conclusion that because of the deceased's age, in all probability he was dead even though no evidence of his death could be found.

I

# THE DEAR OLD PRU ALWAYS PAYS OUT

The genuine appreciation I would receive from my customers when I knocked on their doors was one of extreme gratitude and relief on their behalf because I was the bearer of a most welcome cheque for an amount a wife had insured her husband in the event of his death. Frequently many a wife on seeing such an amount her face would light up in joyful elation. "The dear old Pru always pay out don't they?" one such wife was heard to say and she was really pleased that I had persuaded her and her husband to increase his life assurance twelve months before. "I honestly don't know how I'd have managed to pay all the bills" she remarked with the utmost sincerity. I am sure Prudential agents all over the country must have been told similar stories countless times over many years. I also felt that the personal satisfaction I received on paying out on all death claims was most satisfying in view of the circumstances. At times I felt I was doing a sort of community service for the general public by handing over a cheque to some family which had been absolutely shattered by the death of a loved one.

I know that whatever the amount of insurance money is paid out for the loss of that loved one, it will never compensate for such a tragedy which will bring much mourning and sadness to a family. I believe a payment at such a time from an insurance company, however distressing for all concerned will help considerably by easing any financial difficulties they may have. This therefore is to me what having a life assurance policy is all about as it does bring a certain amount of security in the event of a death. It is at that particular time the last thing one wants is to have financial difficulties and The Prudential, to my knowledge, had built up a reputation of trust, honesty and fairness which made them such a great company. Only very rarely did the Pru refuse to pay out on a death claim. I must have completed hundreds of death claim forms over the years and apart from one claim, which was very untrustworthy, I cannot remember any others. As that woman remarked "The dear old Pru always pay out don't they"? I couldn't possibly improve on that.

# MICHAEL'S PENSION POLICY

Michael was usually a thoroughly nice man until it came for him to pay his yearly Prudential pension policy. When he was in his forties, I had persuaded him to have this type of policy and being self-employed he would qualify for tax relief which at the time appealed to him. He was a confirmed bachelor who lived with his parents and although he liked the opposite sex and had many lady friends, he was never the marrying type. At times he could be a heavy drinker so it would be perhaps rather difficult for any woman to be married to him. Because of the life-style he led he was never able to save much money. I was concerned for him that when retirement came along, apart from the old age state pension he would hardly have enough to live on. Finally, after many months of trying to convince him of the necessity of having this type of policy, he relented and actually wrote out a cheque for the first year's premium. Getting Michael to have this policy had been quite a challenge and I was naturally pleased that I had succeeded. At his age it made sense to start planning for his future being self-employed and single. I used to tell him that if he didn't start looking after himself then no-one else would.

Every year over a period of twenty years I would inform Michael that his yearly premium for his Prudential pension renewal was due. Talk about trying to sell ice-creams to Eskimos this was far worse as he so clearly resented having to pay this premium. What didn't help either was that his drinking pals had told him that for him to have a private pension was a complete waste of time. Being overweight he would probably have a heart attack and never live to draw his pension. So to hear such comments had a very unpleasant effect on him as he constantly grumbled that he should never have allowed himself to have such a policy. One might well ask why did I tolerate him as I certainty wouldn't have taken such behaviour from anyone else. The reason was simple enough really as Michael was my brother and five years senior to me. Being such a poor scholar right from his school days (I wasn't much better) I sort of felt very protective of him being the only son of my parents' four boys who never married. Consequently most of his life he lived with his parents. When our Father died and later when our Mother became ill, he took it upon himself to look after her by taking early retirement. He really dedicated his life to her and for three long years he did a fantastic job of looking after her and rarely left her side. His patience was most extraordinary and Mother said before she died that no Mother could have had a better son. So when Michael was inclined to lose his temper with me and would actually throw his cheque book at me to write out the cheque for his pension, I took all his grumbling in my stride. I was immensely indebted to him for such love and tender care which he gave to our Mother.

Finally, after twenty years of paying his private pension with the Pru, the time was right for him to draw his pension and during those twenty years I had actually encouraged him to increase his premiums a couple of times to give him an even better pension. He did reluctantly, probably to keep me off his back, but I was only interested in his financial state when he could at last draw his pension and didn't his policy pay dividends for him when he realised what amount he was going to draw once a month. What he couldn't understand was that after just a few years The Prudential was paying him far more than he had ever paid in. He then said to me "that pension The Prudential is paying me is incredible and it is the best investment I have ever done". Considering all the hassle I had taken from him was, indeed, a compliment. At the age of sixty-nine Michael died having drawn his Prudential pension for nearly six years. The pleasing aspect for me though was that because he had no financial problems in his retirement he was happy and contented.

# CHIEF OFFICE

When I visited the Prudential Chief Office in Holborn Bars, London, it always left a profound impression with me. The magnificence of the building would repeatedly leave a sense of pride in me that I was employed by such a company. Its headquarters' known as Chief Office was such an imposing structure which suited the Prudential's financial profile in keeping with its status as a national institution.

The building was partly built in 1879 when plans had been made to extend it, but it then took 20 years for the building to be finally completed. It has dominated the Holborn street scene ever since the building was a victory for a good relationship between the Prudential's board of Directors and Alfred Waterhouse who was a highly successful London Architect, who was commissioned to design the building. This architect was known across the country for his distinctive style and had a vision of what was required for a much bigger and grander building.

Besides being an early office development the Prudential's Chief Office was among the largest privately initiated building ventures in London at the turn of the century and became a landmark in the capital. Its 166-foot tower and spire and crow-stepped roofs had a paler shade of red covering the whole of the building with its Victorian gothic inspired features that marked the facade such as turrets, parapets, double lanced windows with its great pointed archway entrance made this beautiful building a character all of its own.

If the building was imposing from the outside, then the interior was equally impressive, where some areas were decorated and furnished to the highest standard. Where windows and doors bore gothic leaded tracery, most noticeable was the oak panelling of some corridors with marble walls and floors with many decorative features from a variety of architectural styles. The company boardroom was extraordinarily striking, as one would anticipate from a company of its size, where major decisions would have been made over many years. By the early 1900s there were 2,000 people employed there, which increased to at least double with the substantial growth of the Prudential.

The Figure of Prudence bearing the image 0f cardinal virtue
which became the Company Seal

Prudential field staff in an unidentified part of the country. Note
the number of women. Taken in 1890.

Prudential agents from Leeds, taken in 1902

The Prudential chief office was completed in 1906. This
magnificent building has dominated the  Holborn Scene ever since.

The unveiling in 1922 of the War Memorial to Prudential staff in
the courtyard of Chief Office who died in the first World War

A soldier, who is about to depart in wartime to the Front, has assured his life and has made proper provision for his dependants who are his wife and his mother.

Disasters often brought out the gallantry of Prudential agents. Here is an agent helping a policy holder to safety in the floods of 1953 in Eastern England

## Prudential Assurance Company, Ltd.
### HOLBORN BARS, LONDON.

# 'TITANIC' DISASTER.
### 14th April, 1912.

Claims have already been paid by this Company in respect of

## 292 PERSONS
*(262 of the Crew and 30 Passengers)*

who lost their lives in this disaster. The total amount paid
to date is

# £12,834.

*9th May, 1912.*　　　　　　　　　A. C. THOMPSON, *General Manager.*

The sinking of the Titanic in 1912 resulted in the loss of 1,513 lives,
nearly one fifth of which were insured with Prudential.

The Stamford district of the Prudential in 1964 which included agents, wives and staff members, visiting the Chief Office. The author is second row far right and his wife Kathleen is sitting second right front row.

Spalding District 1984, Mr George Wallder , district manager, sitting centre second row, with staff members and wives on a visit to Chief Office in 1983.
The author is on the back, seventh from the right.

Prudential in Asia. After more than a decade of vigorous sustained growth , Prudential has become Asia's leading European based Life Insurer as well as a major player in Asia's Fund Management Sector. Prudential has become the financial provider of choice for over 10 million customers in markets across Asia.

# A LESSON LEARNED

Let me say straight away that an incident I'm going to mention in this chapter happened well before the breathalyser came into existence so to my knowledge I was hardly breaking the law. In today's society, however, one should never drink and drive because the consequences of such an act can be catastrophic.

One hundred yards from my home was my last call of the evening where a policy was maturing on one of my clients. I had deliberately left this call for 8 pm as my client, whom I knew well, might persuade me to partake in a drink with him. So it made good sense to leave my car as near to my home as possible. Now I knew from experience that when a policy finishes the claimant might be so pleased with the money he is about to draw that as a way of celebration he might indulge in a glass of whisky. I was always well aware of what could happen if I was offered a drink so I would strictly abide to the rule of one drink being quite sufficient and then I'd be off. Sure enough when the man knew how much he was going to draw, he was delighted and expressed much pleasure. He then remarked "let's have a drink to celebrate" and having persuaded him to take out another policy which would replace the one maturing I was feeling quite pleased with myself and willing to oblige. Once the whisky bottle appeared he was forever topping up my drink at all too frequent intervals. Now I knew this couldn't continue and made my excuses and left despite his protests that I should have another. I then drove my car the one hundred yards home being quite capable of driving. I certainly didn't feel worse for wear and well in control of myself.

Having written that I would strictly abide to have just one drink if offered one, I realised that because of the generosity of my client and near neighbour, I allowed him to top up my glass. Purely because I was so very close to my home and what I learned later that evening was never to be tempted again, the reason being I was violently ill and couldn't stop myself from being sick, not that I'd eaten much because I hadn't and most of that night I felt dreadful and hardly slept all night. The next day I had applied for a day's holiday in order to play for my club, Peterborough Town, in a cricket match against Northants Amateurs who were always a good side often with ex-professionals in their team. However, I was in no condition to play in this match and because it was a midweek fixture, if I did drop out the team would struggle to find a replacement at such a late stage. So it meant it was imperative I would have to play but I still felt I should inform the skipper how ill I felt. However, I didn't have time as the skipper told me to pad up as our team were batting. So here I was walking to the wicket with my fellow opening batsman feeling utterly terrible and seriously questioned myself what I was doing there.

As regards my cricket, I've never had much to boast about as at times I've been very ordinary. Just occasionally, however, everything might just come together and this particular day was one such day because just about every ball I faced was hit in the middle of the bat. Normally I might suffer with nerves but I felt too ill to be nervous as I was deliberately trying to get myself out, in view of how I felt as the ball was being repeatedly hammered to the boundary. I've always said it was the best innings I ever played, scoring seventy-nine runs in just over an hour against a very good bowling attack. Later that day and still feeling ill, the skipper allowed me to leave early and on getting home I retired to my bed.

The following morning I felt fine, cheerfully greeting my customers without a care in the world as I would sing "Oh what a beautiful mornin'". During that day I would often reflect on my innings of a lifetime and could I ever play an innings like that again? At the cost of feeling that ill once more, no I wouldn't. It was a lesson learned.

# HOW THE OTHER HALF LIVES

Before I write anything detrimental for which I may have cause to regret, I must write that just occasionally I would visit some homes where I would find unbelievable squalor on a large scale. As I am not mentioning names, I feel that this book wouldn't be complete without writing about how the other half live. To be perfectly honest, it is indeed only a small fraction of the community that I called on because a good 90% of the people were spotlessly clean. So much so that some of those highly polished kitchen floors were clean enough to eat from. To visit such homes was my delight to be in such a clean and comfortable environment and if I was having difficulties trying to sell a policy and was in for the long haul, which could take some considerable time, I would at least be in a friendly and clean home however long the sale took to complete. There is always the exception though and I mean the other side of the coin and where I would be very apprehensive of what I was about to see.

How can one describe the filthiest homes imaginable where I have always struggled to come to terms? Where I would come across such a scene of gruesome degradation, where I just couldn't comprehend how people could live in such contemptible places. Try to imagine such a scene where windows hadn't been cleaned for years with grubby looking curtains full of holes and thick layers of muck and dust covering all the furniture. Where walls being nearly black and no decorating done for decades and in those so called living rooms there was hardly ever a carpet down. The kitchens were disgusting places where weeks of dirty washing waiting to be washed literally piled up against the wall, with scores of unclean dinner plates filling up the kitchen sink waiting to be washed and a polluted looking cooker creating repulsive uncleanliness of a colossal scale. Amongst the sickening and vile smell of stale urine and the smell of human bodies who hadn't washed themselves properly for weeks. Yes some people did live that way.

So when I was collecting premiums from such homes, I had this fear of never venturing any further than the front door. If there was the possibility of further business in those types of homes, however, I would swallow my pride and enter irrespective of the conditions. Once inside it was impossible to find a clean chair to sit on as all chairs would be heavily stained by grease or anything else I might be sitting on. I well remember one such incident when I first joined The Prudential and was quite pleased with myself that I'd sold an I.B. policy. Because of concentrating on the proposal form, I had accepted a cup of tea. Without thinking I gulped the tea down without bothering to look at the cup. On finishing the cup I thought there was a strange taste and by looking in the cup it was absolutely filthy and much stained. I couldn't believe I had allowed myself to drink from such a cup and for many weeks afterwards I felt positively sick just thinking about it. So I did learn from that incident and that was never drink a cup of tea in such foul and dirty places. Usually I would be in and out of such places as quickly as I could and being in the fresh air again felt really beautiful to breathe properly again. In view of the squalid circumstances I had encountered, for the rest of the day I would be scratching at my body and only felt clean again by having a hot bath on arriving home.

# SHOCKED BEYOND BELIEF

The telephone rang and the lady spoke in such a posh business-like manner and told me I had been recommended to her by a friend. The lady, being a farmer's wife who wanted to insure the building and contents of her farmhouse, and would I call on her. Obviously never having met the lady, I was intrigued by her voice and could this be a rich man's farmer's wife as I was already thinking of the possibility of even more business. It was a wet and cold winter's evening and the farm took some finding in rural Lincolnshire. So on arriving at the farm I rang the bell on the farm gate and about a dozen dogs leapt into action. They were barking and snarling on seeing me on the other side of the gate in their quest to get to me. So here I am standing at the farm gate in a very apprehensive mood as to what could happen when the gate was opened. Eventually the farmer's wife appeared and unlocked the gate with the dogs leaping up and down, being their way of greeting me. The farmer's wife tried to convince me that the dogs were harmless and only wanted to be friendly. I had heard such talk before, however, as I got as close to her as possible as we walked into the farmhouse.

Inside the farmhouse what I saw took me completely by surprise as over many years I had visited many farms and generally all of them were as clean as any other home. This farmhouse was not only filthy with rubbish strewn all over the place, but with the most repulsive of smells going up my nostrils making me feel sick. I was asked to sit down providing I could find a seat amongst so much untidiness as I gently lowered myself onto an armchair which was under many cardboard boxes. Guess what? Up pops a chicken! I had already seen chickens in that living room with many cats also. I did manage to write up the business, having declined the usual offering in such places for a cup of tea. I did wonder later if the farmhouse would turn out to be a bad risk because just one spark would have set everywhere up in flames and looking as though a bomb had hit it.

On escorting me back to the farm gate, the farmer's wife, again surrounded by the dogs, and as a way of making conversation I asked the woman how many dogs they had. "At the last count it was fourteen" she informed me. Out of curiosity I remarked "Where do they sleep at night?" It was probably a silly question because I naturally assumed the dogs would be sleeping on the farm somewhere and probably being good guard dogs "They all sleep in the bedroom with me and my husband" she answers. "Surely not all the dogs sleep in the bedroom" I say. "Yes, it's true. Some sleep on the bed with us, some sleep under the bed and the rest are scattered around the bedroom" she replied.

It so happened the evening was bitterly cold and raining and the dogs were soaking wet. It is hard to believe that those fourteen dogs would finish up in the bedroom and heaven knows what that bedroom looked like. Often in my work as an insurance man I could be really shocked and on hearing that remark, was one such occasion. I was shocked beyond belief.

# AS DIFFERENT AS CHALK AND CHEESE

After serving my first ten years with The Prudential on a rather small and at times an unproductive agency where any success I may have had was very limited, so it was that I yearned for a better and bigger agency where there would be more potential for me to sell the company's policies which would increase my earnings capability. I already knew I was a good enough salesman to sell the company's I.B. policies as my results in the Stamford district production list proved. I wanted to expand more, however, by selling more of the company's O.B. and G.B. policies. I always felt this was not possible on my first agency as the potential for finding such new clients was very restricted.

Then an opportunity came along when an established and high profile agency became vacant at Market Deeping. I immediately applied for it as I knew that providing I put in the necessary work involved, I would definitely obtain a better standard of living for my wife and two young children. So I was ecstatic that my application was successful and couldn't wait to start. In many ways, however, I was very upset to leave my old agency in view of the many friends I had made with my Prudential customers over those ten years. Strangely enough I did feel guilty about leaving them as they had accepted such a shy and inexperienced young insurance man into their homes and where I had been made so very welcome. So when I said goodbye, I felt I was letting them down particularly after all the cups of tea I had enjoyed with them. I would particularly miss my old friend Janet's scrumptious home-made fish and chips which she cooked for me every Friday evening as I was just too busy to dash home for something to eat. It was, therefore, a sad time as more than once I had a tear in my eye on saying that final and conclusive goodbye.

The time spent on my first agency was, I believe, invaluable. I felt it was an apprenticeship for what was to come and the experience gained would hold me in good stead for the change I was about to make. What I wouldn't miss was all the chasing about on Friday evenings and some Saturday mornings to collect the I.B. premiums from my bad payers. I hoped eventually they would be just a blur on the memory. I believe I would have moved literally anywhere for a different agency and being ambitious I wanted to test myself more. The new agency was just six miles north of my first agency and I would be required to live in Market Deeping, which was fairly central to all the areas I'd be covering on my new patch. So it meant selling up in Werrington where as a family we had lived for five years and moving house to Market Deeping. Suddenly the nervous system within me flared up again and I was having grave misgivings as to whether I was capable of taking such a high profile agency. Also, would I be accepted by my new customers where there were many hundreds of them I was yet to meet? Say if I appeared incompetent and simply unable to deal with the many problems I would encounter with such a large agency. The general branch was colossal with many lorries, motor cars and hundreds of house insurance policies to look after which would test a man with far superior knowledge of the insurance industry than me. I was having last minute doubts but what I did know was that once on that new agency I would give it my absolute all and surely no-one could have asked for more.

I would be working in a country area with the majority of my customers living in Market Deeping and Deeping St James and also took in half a dozen villages going north. The agency was approximately ten miles square and considering at that time the Pru had business in one in every five houses, I was going to be a very busy insurance man. When I started my new patch, however, I soon realised that a rural area is vastly different to a city area and I quickly learned the difference between the two agencies was substantial with the prospect of new business being written up more than in the city area.

What a transformation I was to experience between the two agencies just six miles apart but which were as different as chalk and cheese. With regard to my weekly I.B. collections I hardly had any bad payers with only a handful to call back on in the evenings. Customers on my new agency seemed more insurance minded and more interested when I spoke about a further policy, where on my previous agency it was often an achievement to get them to listen to me.

Some of my customers on my new agency had lived in the villages all their lives so they could go back a long way with regard to many Prudential insurance agents calling on them. In the early days I was repeatedly told to be compared with my predecessors I had a lot to learn, where such insurance men were of high moral standards and so very well respected in the community. I was told "you will never be as good as the previous insurance men who called on us". One such insurance man was not only exceptional in the amount of new business he achieved every year that he was a regular star dinner attendee as a reward for his new business produced. This particular agent was a fine man in everything he did and in every house I called on no-one could say a bad work about him. He would go shopping for his elderly customers who couldn't get out, would gladly take the ill to the health centre or hospital and even took one elderly couple who hadn't a car, down to London Heathrow for their holiday abroad and be there for their return home. I had got a lot to live up to and only time would tell if I was to be a success or not.

Looking back to my previous agency I had faced a similar situation. I had followed a well-liked insurance agent who had retired but had gradually won over my customers by being myself, which I believe is the only way to be. By all means learn from your predecessors how they had earned such reverence from their customers but I had to be my own man and if I did fail I'd only have myself to blame.

# LIFE INSPECTORS

Life inspectors were a special breed in The Prudential field staff and were looked upon as the elite salesmen of the company, the cream as it were who were proven salesmen having worked their way up the promotion ladder and showed a particular flair for selling. They would turn up on an agent's doorstep looking immaculately dressed and every inch the man from the Pru with their brief-case at the ready. The policies they would sell were the ordinary branch policies of the company's business. The life inspector would have many different policies to sell and these included life assurance, savings plans, pensions, bonds, ISA's, annuities and numerous other policies at his disposal. With regard to the selling of Prudential policies the majority of life inspectors I ever worked with were good but as in all professions some were better than others, the occasional one being brilliant with others being average. I was most fortunate to have worked with some of the best where nothing would be too much trouble and who were prepared to call at any given address in the relentless pursuit of writing up new business.

Every district throughout the country would have a permanent life inspector and roughly once a month the agent was programmed for a day with him. Therefore, it was the agent's absolute responsibility to find a certain amount of appointments for that day. He would accompany the life inspector on most of the appointments made as a way of introducing him to every potential client visited. Also just about all the O.B. policies were paid by direct debit which obviously meant less collecting of premiums at the door. Any commission earned from the sale of these policies were shared with the life inspector, which was fair enough as his earnings for the month would be worked out entirely on the amount of new business he had completed. So it really was to the benefit of both the agent and the life inspector that they had a successful day.

The day allotted with the life inspector could be a constant worry for the agent to find the necessary appointments and at times he would be under much pressure. When I was programmed with him, I tried to get at least half a dozen calls, preferably where the client could afford that bigger premium and where a good life inspector was more than capable of achieving, being a specialist in that department. I also had a number of calls in reserve just in case the appointments didn't produce any business. I know I had my own register of all the customers on my books which I would continually be searching but how many times could one keep going back to Prudential policy holders hoping they might agree to have another policy. Surely though one can only get so much blood out of a stone as it really was a worrying time for the agent, who obviously didn't want to disappoint the life inspector with a programme of unsatisfactory appointments where the prospect of writing up new business was virtually nil.

I think I was most fortunate that for a number of years I had as my life inspector Tony Smith who was not only a good salesman but a firm friend. Luckily for me he lived in Market Deeping so it was to my advantage to use him quite regularly, not just when I was programmed with him but other times also when I would visit him. Also by telephone informing him to see one such person with whom I thought there was the possibility of some new business. I felt we gelled together very well indeed, so much so we could sniff a call out of nothing. Over the many years I worked with Tony, I cannot remember having a blank day when working together. Looking back now we had many successful times and when the business of the day was done we would retire to the local pub and reflect on the new policies completed, raising our beer glasses by saying "Cheers" to another successful day.

# HEAD-ON COLLISION

The worst and most worrying claim I had to deal with which caused me to have many sleepless nights with the added fear that I could lose my job through my own incompetence was by far the blackest period I experienced in the whole of my insurance career. Having dealt with literally hundreds of different types of claims this particular one was the most serious, where a motor car which I had only insured just a couple of days before, was involved in a head-on collision with another vehicle. Three people were instantly killed who had only just sailed into this country from Holland that morning, having disembarked an hour earlier at Harwich, Suffolk, only to be killed on British roads.

Having insured this motor car only hours previously, this terrifying motor accident made me realise what a huge claim it was going to be. A young man in his early twenties, whom I knew quite well, had been in touch with me to say he wished to insure his newly purchased motor car with The Prudential. Being the age he was, all insurance companies are genuinely nervous when it comes to young drivers, so on the proposal I took down all the necessary details about him and he also told me his nineteen-year-old girlfriend, who had just passed her driving test, wanted to be a named driver on the policy. I then issued him with a cover note and collected the deposit and posted the proposal form to my general branch office at Lincoln. Everything seemed as normal as it possibly could be and I thought no more of it as with my wife and the two children we were off to Chester for the weekend.

On arriving home three days later, first thing Monday morning I received a telephone call from this same young man who informed me there had been a dreadful motor car accident when his young girlfriend was driving his car near Harwich. It was involved in a head-on collision with another car on the Sunday and that three Dutchmen had died in the other car. The young girl driver suffered multiple injuries and was in hospital for months with both vehicles being write-offs. I immediately telephoned the Lincoln claims department of this horrific road accident.

The claim dragged on for over a year because the three men killed were all employed in management position where they earned excellent salaries and were all married with young children and had big mortgages on their homes in Holland. This information was obviously going to make the claim very substantial and in excess of £300,000 pounds. At the inquest the young girl driver was proved to be guilty so The Prudential admitted liability and met the claim in full. Even though the claim was settled, I was in serious trouble not just because of the size of the claim, but by a terrible oversight by me. I had not got the young man's signature on the proposal form and without his signature The Prudential could evidently have fought the claim which would have saved the company many thousands of pounds. Because of this I was interviewed by three senior claims inspectors from Lincoln where I was informed I was in serious trouble so I really did fear the worst. Being at that time 46 years of age and if my company had dispensed with my services, my chances of being employed elsewhere in the insurance industry were virtually nil.

One morning just over a year from the date of the accident, I was sent for by the divisional manager in Nottingham. That car journey to Nottingham was the worst car journey I have ever done. Was I really going to lose my job I repeatedly kept asking myself? If so, how would I be able to support my family and how could I possibly find the same enjoyment in any other occupation. I had blown it and I only had myself to blame. I tried to console myself that things could be worse. Far worse, in fact. Say if I had cancer with only weeks to live, surely that was worse than losing my job. So many thoughts were going through my mind and if I did lose my job the only consolation would be that I would finally know the outcome as I had lived with this motor claim for over a year - a rather tortuous year as there was not a day went by without me thinking of the consequences of what my fate would be. Would I be dismissed or not as the day of reckoning had surely arrived.

It was a very nervous agent who presented himself at the divisional office that day. To my surprise, the divisional manager greeted me warmly in the relaxed atmosphere of his office. He could not have been friendlier but it did cross my mind that he was deliberately softening me up for the dreaded news that I half expected to hear. To my great surprise he was very sympathetic towards me and actually admitted that the last twelve months must have been very worrying for my wife and me. He then informed me that my district manager at Stamford had spoken well of me and because of that my job was safe. The relief I felt on hearing those words was considerable, as if a heavy weight I had carried for months was finally lifted from me. I realised also that it was my good fortune to have Mr Ernest Rodgers as my district manager as it was precisely that which he had said about me that I was not dismissed. I do not like to speak ill of the other seven district managers I served under in my time with the Pru, but would they have taken my side the way Mr Rodgers did? Of that I will never know.

On walking along Maid Marion Way in Nottingham to collect my car, I was on such a high I felt I was floating on air. If my car journey to Nottingham that morning was the worst car journey I could ever remember, then the return journey to Market Deeping was the sweetest. I couldn't wait to tell Kathleen, who I knew was just as worried as me. Most importantly, I was still "The man from the Pru". I felt completely rejuvenated. Could my life have possibly been any better at that time on driving home? I very much doubt it.

# SLEEP WALKING

I didn't realise when I joined The Prudential that years later I would be in a hotel in London and I would be very apprehensive of what might happen to me during the night as I was forced to stay awake when being part of the Stamford district when about 20 staff members had spent the day at Chief Office, Holborn bars. That evening my hotel bedroom was on the 7th floor and it turned out to be the hottest night of the year. So before getting into bed I opened the bedroom windows for the fresh air to float in. Then just as I was dropping off to sleep I suddenly realised why on earth I had opened the windows in view of what had happened just a few months before. So I got out of bed and closed the windows and even locked them even though it was such a humid summer's night. I had good reason to lock those windows, however, because just months before I had got out of bed at home at 2 am and was trying desperately to open my bedroom window in order to get out of the house. That night in London the incident had come back to haunt me with the genuine fear that seven floors up I would jump out of the window to certain death. So I forced myself to stay awake all night with the fear that I would start walking in my sleep.

A friend of mine years ago was a sleep walker and one night got out of bed, opened the bedroom window and jumped on his motor car and broke both his legs. In my particular instance, I had never had problems like walking in my sleep but about this time the outcome of the head-on collision still had not been settled. With the constant fear of losing my job hanging over me and with not sleeping at all well, I believe the terrible road accident was playing on my mind far more than I ever realised. I think what came to my rescue that night at home was that we had recently had new double glazed windows installed throughout the house and as the windows were unfamiliar to me, I couldn't open them. Under the circumstances, this was just as well. What also came to my rescue was that Kathleen, because of the noise I was making, had woken up and started shouting at me as to what I was doing. I seemed completely oblivious to any noise I was making by banging on the windows. By this time Kathleen had got out of bed and calmed me down with me waking up and returning to my bed and normality.

I know many years later and looking back I hadn't a clue as to what I was doing that night and in my subconscious mind I had no control of mind or body. The night I spent in that London hotel I was paralysed with fear that if I allowed myself to sleep, I just wouldn't have the necessary control over myself if I started to walk in my sleep. The consequences were just too horrific to contemplate and being 7 floors up I was not tempting providence as to what might happen.

# MAD DOGS AND AN ENGLISHMAN

Noel Coward, English actor, dramatist, author, composer of light music wrote and sung in 1932 "Mad dogs and Englishmen go out in the midday sun". His description of this light-hearted song fits in perfectly with this Englishman when I ventured out in the midday sun. When knocking on endless doors, I have to say that an insurance man's enemy was the family dog and I have had many skirmishes with some really savage-looking beasts and literally fighting for my life a couple of times as they would try to bite lumps out of me and often succeeded. Some dogs may be a man's best friend but for an insurance man it was an animal to avoid at all costs. This was most evident with me when knocking on a door as at that precise moment these animals would go berserk with much barking and snarling from the other side of the door. I was often in fear of what could happen if the dog was somehow let loose so because of this I had to be permanently on my guard on knocking on some doors. Where at times there would be a dog of such a violent nature that I would be wobbling at the knees and sweating profusely. What would often amaze me was that the bigger the dog, the smaller the house where they would spend most of their time. With the poor things stuck indoors virtually all day, little wonder the only excitement the dog would get was when that nervous-looking insurance man came knocking on the door.

Two instances I am never likely to forget concerning dogs, both being Alsatians, and normally at one particular call the woman of the house would slightly open her front door just enough for her money and insurance books to be passed to me amid much growling by her dog. Now the collection of the premiums at this house had always gone reasonably well until one day when the woman was not at home and it was her husband who opened the door to me. Yes, wide open. This then was the opportunity of a lifetime for this Alsatian to take some form of revenge against this person who comes once a month to disturb the dog's morning sleep by knocking on the front door. The dog couldn't believe its luck by taking a flying jump at me with such force that I was knocked backwards onto the lawn at the front of the house. I dread to think what might have happened if there had been concrete that my head fell on and not grass, which obviously softened the blow. At that very moment this big fearsome-looking dog was on top of me as I wrestled with it on the grass. Sensing the kill, it proceeded to bite me but, fortunately, what came to my rescue was my insurance collecting book. When I am collecting premiums it is always with me and by pushing this book repeatedly into the jaws of this ferocious-looking dog, I was able to fight the dog off me. Eventually the husband was able to get control of his dog but it was a close call. Afterwards I was in considerable shock at what had happened and finished up in hospital for treatment, my one consolation being it could have been much worse.

The other incident was equally as frightful as I had received a telephone call from my district office that someone wished to see me at the local caravan site with a view hopefully to writing up some business. I was told that when I found the caravan, to stay in my car and keep tooting the car horn and the owner of the caravan would come out to see me. I was also told that under no circumstances was I to leave my car as the owner had a vicious Alsatian dog which doesn't take to strangers knocking on the caravan door - so with this information in mind I found the caravan and sitting in my car started tooting my car horn. I could by this time see the dog well chained up by the side of the caravan and barking its head off. I still kept tooting my car horn but there seemed no movement whatsoever from inside the caravan. After about 5 minutes with still no-one coming to see me, I decided that as the dog was chained up then no way could it attack me. I decided it would be safe for me to leave my car and knock on the caravan door. What a mistake that proved to be as I was savagely attacked by this huge Alsatian dog.

Halfway between my car and the caravan, the dog somehow broke its lead with me being halfway to nowhere. I realised straight away how utterly foolish I had been as I had been warned to stay in my car. I had disregarded that blatant warning and this time I was totally unprepared for such an attack as I hadn't got my collecting book or brief-case with which to defend myself. I felt so vulnerable and very much at the mercy of this dog, snarling and showing its enormous teeth as it attacked its prey and bit my leg. Fortunately the owner of the caravan decided to make his appearance and managed to get hold of his dog. The owner of the dog was hardly sympathetic to my cause, however, by saying "Didn't you get my message from your office that under no circumstances were you to leave your car and wait for me to come out of my caravan"? I told him I had sat in my car for 5 minutes and kept tooting my car horn but he wasn't listening. I wasn't going to argue with him as blood was seeping through my trouser leg and once again I found myself going to the hospital for treatment.

On reflection I suppose I was partly to blame and should have stayed in my car longer but when I saw the dog chained up I wrongly assumed it couldn't attack me. I really was a victim of Noel Coward's hilariously funny "Mad dogs and Englishmen go out in the midday sun". Yes I've been there and done that. Talk about being eaten alive, it can happen.

# BY THEIR OWN HAND

I've known a few suicides working in the insurance industry and four such deaths of a self-inflicted nature by my customers I can clearly remember. This most delicate of subjects causes me to be apprehensive about writing about this, but it would be wrong of me not to mention a topic that I did occasionally come across as an insurance agent. Dark forces within a person can cause much devastation in quite an overwhelming and immovable way by taking one's own life when the mind is frightfully disturbed and where such dark forces can literally control one's life by a variety of means. The anxiety of one's health problems to financial hardship and unemployment or an unhappy marriage are but a few of the reasons for self-destruction. So one has to come to the conclusion that an individual must be in a very confused and depressed state of mind to contemplate the suicide option of ending one's life.

I do not propose to mention how three of my customers took their own lives only to say it was in a most violent way. The four people mentioned did have one thing in common and that was depression, which eats right into the heart and soul of these unfortunate people. We should never for one moment criticise any individual for taking their own life but show profound sympathy and compassion. How would we react in similar circumstances when for some of these people it would be quite an effort even to get through a whole day? I always felt really remorseful when I had to deal with a death claim where the life assured had taken his own life. For the families in some instances it would be nearly too much to bear that a beloved member of their family had died in such a way. It always left a great air of despondency in the houses that I called on. One of the four mentioned who took his own life was an old friend going back over forty years who took it upon himself to starve to death. Little did I think that seeing him in the local health centre a month before he died that it would be the last time I would see him. Strangely enough, I shouldn't have been too surprised in learning of his death because in his depressed state of mind he had threatened to do just that.

I believe my friend's troubles began when he took early retirement in his early sixties but once retired I began to see a marked deterioration in him as he seemed to have no interests and little motivation to try to get involved in anything. I also sensed that his wife was becoming increasingly more worried as time went by. He was always a man who carried little weight whatsoever so when his health declined he looked thinner than ever. He looked far from well as his depression began to overtake him. It was about this time when I saw him in the health centre as he had made an appointment to see his doctor. Sitting next to him in the reception he rather casually informed me that because of his depressed state he was suicidal and had lost the will to live. I really did feel the worse for him and just looking at him I knew he was very serious indeed. So to be told such a thing from a person whom I'd known for so many years shook me as I tried to tell him he had everything to live for and not to do anything silly. I meant every word but he just wasn't listening.

A few weeks later I saw his wife and naturally enquired how her husband was only to be told he had died. Evidently the day I saw him in the health centre the doctor was worried about his condition and he was admitted to hospital. From there his deterioration got worse as he literally refused to eat anything that was put in front of him. He couldn't be persuaded by anyone to change his mind. They tried to pump liquid food into his body but he wasn't having that either. So my friend and customer took his own life because he had lost the will to live any more. I for one was extremely sorrowful to hear of his death which must surely be one of the worst ways of self-destruction possible so I conclude that when he took his own life his mind was in turmoil when he came to such a tragic decision to end his life. That is what depression can do for a person.

# MARATHONS AND SPONSORSHIP

One of the advantages of being the local man from the Pru was that I was reasonably well known which I exploited to my advantage when I was in training for one of my marathon walks. So as I was seeing many of my customers either weekly or monthly it was the ideal opportunity for me to ask them to sponsor me, which invariably they did. My walking had started in 1986 while on holiday in Spain as I had started to put on weight. With the cricket season fast approaching I knew that if I didn't help myself, I wouldn't be able or fit enough to continue to play the game. So on returning home from Spain, having discovered the joys of walking, I started to walk anything from 5 to 10 miles a day which left me considerably slimmer than before. Frequently I would rise early and even walk a few miles before I started work. The sheer pleasure of being out early in the morning in the countryside where I live left a deep and lasting impression on me. With the sun coming up and walking amongst the startled rabbits with birds twittering merrily away took some beating. It always gave me a good to be alive feeling and it was on my morning walk that an inspiration came to me. Why not put all this walking to good use by raising money for charities? So this is what happened and this meant extending my walking to be fit enough to walk marathons and at the same time asking people to sponsor me. I had to be careful, however, that these extra commitments did not interfere with my work and, fortunately, I managed to combine the two quite successfully.

I participated in one marathon a year and over a period of 14 years I completed fourteen marathons, being 6 London marathons, 6 local marathons and 2 in

America, the Boston and the New York City marathon. The personal satisfaction I gained by completing those marathons was exhilarating, so much so that nothing I have accomplished in life before or since stands comparison. The elation of raising substantial amounts of money by people sponsoring me for charity is something I will never forget. It is The Prudential, however, I have to thank and not because they always gave me a good sized cheque on completing a marathon, but also to thank the Pru because if it wasn't for them I couldn't possibly have raised the money I did. Half of all the people who sponsored me over 14 years were Prudential policyholders, in other words my customers. They supported me with sponsorship money every time I asked them and I really did have a great relationship with them which has remained to this day.

Having said how thankful I am to The Prudential that I was able to collect certain amounts of money from my customers, there were also many friends, small businesses, relatives, Rotary clubs, Probus clubs, Women's Institute, Lions club, Cricket club players and Parish Church members of St Guthlac's Church, Market Deeping, just to name a few. What was really appreciated, I would be seen out shopping with my wife or out on the street when dear little old ladies having heard I was in training for another walk would give me £1 or 50p saying they wished they could give more. How very lucky I was to be living in Market Deeping and writing this book gives me the opportunity to thank every single one of them for their generosity. One stipulation I always insisted on keeping was that if I didn't complete any marathon, all 26 miles of them, even with just a mile to go, then any money previously collected would be returned. So the incentive was very much on me to complete all those marathons and it was not for me to blame the endless obstacles I had come across walking

111

those marathons but to get my head down and battle through in order to keep the momentum and concentration going. There was so much at stake considering all those people who had sponsored me so the fear of failing was very deep routed in me and it really was that fear that drove me on.

When I was made redundant aged 58, I was determined even more so to continue walking. What better way in retirement to keep fit in mind and body than to enter marathons, which for me was the ideal exercise as I got older? When it was time to go knocking on doors for a forthcoming marathon was something I really looked forward to doing, particularly on visiting my old customers who continued to sponsor me whichever charity I was promoting. On seeing them again and renewing friendships of years past over that so welcome cup of tea, it meant that nothing had changed. It really was my delight to see them again and that strong bond between us had never been broken. Eventually, as the years progressed and at the age of 67, I reluctantly retired from walking marathons due to a badly damaged ankle. I conceded to the inevitable that my serious walking was in the past but I have two special memories concerning the two marathons I completed in America.

The 2001 New York City marathon was by far the most emotional marathon ever in view of what happened in that great city just 6 weeks before when on September 11 the Twin Towers of the World Trade Centre came crashing down. Terrorists killed nearly 3,000 people and because of this terrible atrocity, 4 million spectators lined the marathon route giving every encouragement to all those competing. For me to walk through the five boroughs of New York was phenomenal with pavements full of well-wishers, with some holding a placard and photograph of a loved one who was lost in the Twin Towers with the words "thanks for doing it for him". At one time because of the security of the marathon it was felt it would be called off but, fortunately, it wasn't and to finish in Central Park, Manhattan, will live with me forever.

My other lasting memory was in 1997 when I completed the Boston marathon in Massachusetts. Approaching the finishing tape after nearly nine hours of walking, and on top of the nearest skyscraper, lighting up the whole of the finish area, was the name "Prudential". How very appropriate that I felt I was coming home.

# THE PRUDENTIAL PAID FOR MY HOLIDAY

When out collecting I.B. premiums one day an elderly woman invited me into her lounge. She wanted a discussion about her three life assurance policies and on handing me the policies she proceeded to say "Brian, I want to visit an old friend in Canada one last time before I die, so which policy can I surrender in order to get some money to pay for my flight". Of the three policies, two were whole life policies and would only be paid out on her death. The remaining policy was a 20 year endowment policy which had been in force for 18 years with just 2 years to the maturity date. The look on her face was rather inquisitive as to what I would be going to say and then I told her that the endowment policy would more than pay for her flight to Canada. In fact, the surrender of the policy was excellent because of the profits earned over 18 years. So she happily surrendered the policy. I then informed her that her life cover left on her life was now inadequate and that the policy now surrendered should be replaced by another and because of her age this would be her last opportunity to have another policy. She willingly agreed to this, meaning that at her age she would be well covered for funeral expenses at her death.

With the arrival of the cheque from the surrender of the policy she was really thrilled with the amount she had received and then said "I've now got even more money to spend on myself". So off she went to Canada for 3 weeks and on her return was ecstatic over the wonderful holiday she'd had. Whenever I saw her she invariably would remark about her holiday and was so grateful for what The Prudential had done for her.

114

With the progressing years, however, she began suffering with dementia and because of her age began to get slightly confused and once said to me "I've got a lot to thank The Prudential for because it was your company which paid for my holiday in Canada". I would try to convince her that she had surrendered one of her policies to pay for her holiday in Canada and then she would look at me in bewilderment, not quite understanding what I had said to her. Before she died in her mid-eighties, she became even more confused and was convinced the Pru had paid for her holiday and had begun telling friends that The Prudential had treated her years ago to a lovely holiday in Canada and would never forget the Pru's generosity.

# WOMEN OF SUBSTANCE

Joan Wake Close in Market Deeping was one of my favourite places to visit and in those flats for the elderly were some of the sweetest of elderly ladies imaginable. If I had accepted a cup of tea in every flat I called on I would have been there all day. Many of these residents had lost their husbands and would often lead a very lonely existence. Therefore, when I knocked on their flat door their welcome was overwhelming, "come in Brian, I've just put the kettle on as I knew it was your day to call, so sit yourself down and make yourself comfortable" was a greeting I often received on walking into their flat. Over a cup of tea I would then indulge in the most delicious biscuits and be spoilt to death. Yet some of these sweet dears would be house-bound, especially in the winter time being unable to venture out of doors on their own. So I would hear of all the local gossip and the many problems they would encounter - family problems, health problems, financial problems and any other problems they cared to mention.

What would often amaze me would be the relationship, or should I say non-relationship, some of these ladies would have with their children. Admittedly some lived many miles away and would only visit their Mother once a year or in some cases not at all. I am not saying for a moment this lack of communication exists with all families as I know it does not as the vast majority care for their parents with much love and devotion. I also knew from my experience of talking to them as they would open their hearts up to me. In all probability I would be the only person they would see that day, apart from the warden of the flats who was named Jane. Every one of the residents spoke so highly of Jane who would visit the residents regularly and if any of them became ill then a doctor would be called immediately.

Not to be forgotten would be some of the experiences these elderly ladies would have lived through during the dark days of the Second World War. It left me full of admiration for the heroism some of them had shown and I could have listened all day to their tales. Some had moved from the London area to Market Deeping to be near their son or daughter as they became more frail with age but it was their experiences during the hard times of the war that always got my attention and over another cup of tea and biscuit I listened. Some had arrived from the east end of London which had been so heavily bombed during the war. Some could recall memories past of being bombed out of their homes more than once where they lost family members and friends as the bombing intensified so much that they wondered if it was their turn next. I heard stories of these women whilst their husbands were fighting in the war of facing the harsh reality of those days where they would scrub floors all day or other menial jobs in order to bring up their children. Some of these women had 4 or 5 children to bring up all on their own. One woman told me her husband was a prisoner of the Japanese and for 4 years had no communication with him, not knowing whether he was dead or alive and had 5 children to look after and feed. So it really was a period of exceptional hardship and indeed bravery as I heard similar stories from many others. My admiration for them surviving such an ordeal was enormous and during the dark days of the war when London was so heavily bombed it was known as the blitz. These women did their utmost to keep the word great in Great Britain and they really were women of substance.

To finish this chapter on women who were born in a different generation to today's existence, their biggest worry by far in their old age was to make sure there life assurance policies were paid up to date. If I was to miss them, they would worry themselves sick that in the event of their death The Prudential wouldn't pay out the full amount. They were so independent and the last thing they would have wanted was to be a burden to their families as the life assurance policy would pay for all the funeral expenses. I think this attitude stems from their background of hardship and suffering they had lived through and never forgotten. Above all else, they wanted that peace of mind in the event of their death and that they would owe absolutely nothing to anyone. It was my privilege to have known such sweet little old ladies who were an inspiration to me and even when I was made redundant I continued to visit many of them and attended their funerals.

# GENERAL BRANCH SERVICING

I had quite a large general branch (GB) connection which meant dealing with many insurance claims so it really was important that I visited the insured in the quickest possible time in the event of a claim. It might be a burnt carpet in the home or a motor car accident so the insured was entitled to expect the type of servicing which The Prudential prided itself on, and for which the company's field staff were so well known and had been built on over many years. Also, hadn't I told my customers rather proudly that the Pru was one of the finest insurance companies for paying out on all types of claims, which not only gave myself that boost of confidence but a real thrill that whatever the claim it would be dealt with fairly and promptly. So I always knew that a good settlement by The Prudential was a feather in my cap which hopefully would not be forgotten by the insured. Because if there was a chance of further business to be done I was in with a shout as the insured might reflect how efficiently and satisfactorily the claim had been dealt with. Good servicing in GB was so relevant because if the insurance agent didn't look after his customers at that time of need, the business would be lost forever when the renewal notices were issued when next due.

When the GB renewals were released once a month I would have as many as 40 renewal notices to deliver to my customers. Providing I collected the renewal premium when due proved to be a nice little earner by way of commission. So it was vitally important for me to visit them as I believed that the personal touch was what a client would be happy with, rather than the renewal arriving by post, where that customer would rarely meet his insurance man. This to me meant a sure way of losing the business as he or she might start looking elsewhere. I know occasionally my customers would look elsewhere which did happen at times but I worked to keep all my clients and that personal touch meant everything, not just to me but my customers as well.

There was a haulage contractor on my agency which at times would have 14 heavy lorries, 3 motor cars, a tractor, his garage and his house which were all insured with The Prudential. At times this kept me extremely busy in the event of a claim which consequently meant I would spend many hours in his home filling in claim forms. I really valued this haulage company as it was easily the biggest single G.B. connection I had. So if the insured telephoned me concerning a claim, I was instantly mobile in my haste to get to his home, where usually it was one of the lorries which had been involved in a road accident. Just to fill in a claim form, where often the police were involved, I had to be so meticulous I always feared that one day I would lose this GB connection as competition from other insurance companies was never far away. I did know that if the insured had scouted around he could have got his vehicles premiums for less, but I know the insured was well satisfied with the service he got from me and was always loyal to The Prudential. It was also some consolation to him that wherever his lorries were on the highways of Great Britain his vehicles were well insured. Also I had a really good relationship with the insured and that always helped.

So keen was I to keep this business and the commission I received from this connection, however, that if the insured had telephoned me in the middle of the night I would have run to his house with my pyjamas still on.

Now that is what I call good service to my customers because who else would be prepared to do just that. Believe that and you will believe anything.

# CHAIRMAN NORMAN MASON

No, he was not chairman of The Prudential Board of Directors or held any chairmanship or management position either. Over a period of 50 years he excelled by being chairman of the Stamford branch of The Prudential staff union, chairman of the Prudential union of divisional council, chairman of the Stibbington Parish Council, chairman of the Helpston Parish Council, chairman of the Helpston Arms houses Committee and chairman of the Cambridgeshire Association of Parish Councils throughout that county. These positions of Chairman where he served with such distinction made Norman Mason a man to be admired and hugely respected by all who came into contact with him. It was at one of the Stamford staff union meetings that I first met him, he being an insurance agent like myself. We immediately became good friends right up to his death in 2007. Norman, being one of the older established agents, was a big help to me in my early days with the Pru and I really looked up to him. During the Second World War, he served in Italy, notably at the Battle of Monte Casino, and was the youngest Sergeant Major in the Northamptonshire Regiment but it was as an outstanding public speaker, who became the best I had ever set eyes on that I admired him so much.

His chairmanship of all the committees he served on was brilliant and watching him closely at those monthly Stamford branch union meetings I learned from him how a good chairman conducts a meeting. Not for him to rush through a meeting as he was most conscious of that person who would not participate much in the meeting and would try to bring them into the proceedings. For those who spoke far too much he had a great knack of putting them down without offending them. He was impartial towards or against no particular person, being firm but fair at every meeting he chaired. He took me once to the quarterly F division union council meeting at Nottingham. In front of a packed audience of delegates from branches all over the F division he was magnificent as at times the meeting became noisy with some delegates very forceful in expressing themselves. A weaker chairman would lose control, but not Norman and no-one was going to bully this chairman about who was in total command. Many years later I was transferred to Spalding district and by this time Norman was retired and I was asked to become chairman of the Spalding branch of the staff union. Sometimes those meetings could become heated and I would often think what Norman would have done in a similar situation. If I did have any success as a chairman, I had learned it from the master.

When Norman retired at age 60, I didn't see so much of him as before although we always kept in touch. Then into his middle seventies he developed Alzheimer's disease and on hearing this I started visiting him again. With his deterioration in health he became more forgetful and over and over he would be repeating himself. One day Lily his wife said to me "Brian would you please tell Norman that he must not worry himself any more about these audits with The Prudential which he used to do as he is worrying himself sick about the next one". Norman had been retired over 15 years when Lily told me this and I began to see a dramatic change in him. He once said to me "Do I know you"? Eventually Lily couldn't look after him any longer finding him very difficult to manage. Norman was admitted into a care home in Peterborough and later to another care home at Bourne where I would take Lily regularly to see him. By this time he was far worse and he found it difficult to recognise anyone. I know Graham his son was most upset that he couldn't have any communication with his father and occasionally Norman would smile when I'd mention the good old days in the Stamford district we had together. He was in a ward with other dementia sufferers and at times there was a lot of shouting going on and poor Norman would sit there expressionless. A few months before he died he was knocked over and broke his arm and he looked a pitiful sight. The last time I saw him about two weeks before he died, he was a shadow of his former self as Alzheimer's had claimed another victim. That brilliant speaker was no more and what Norman had I would not wish on anyone!

For his funeral his family wanted me to say a few words in tribute. A few days before the funeral, however, I was admitted into hospital myself so I was in no condition to attend which I have always regretted. A few years later Kathleen and I attended a funeral and got talking to a couple who were about our age. In conversation I said that before my retirement I was known as "The man from the Pru". The woman then remarked that her insurance man years ago was Norman Mason, describing him as a perfect gentleman. She then said how much I reminded her of Mr Mason. I can only answer that remark by saying no-one has ever paid me a greater compliment.

# THE STREET KIDS

When I visited India for three weeks holidays many years ago I was traumatised by what I saw and it had a dramatic affect that on returning home to concentrate as "The Man from the Pru" was a very arduous task indeed. I simply couldn't get back to any form of normality. As my wife would remark "You're thinking of India again". Seeing the slums of Calcutta I've never forgotten as I saw intolerable poverty on a colossal scale with literally thousands of street kids begging on the streets or scavenging on rubbish tips.

One morning outside my hotel there were dozens of these kids who were pleading with the residents, like myself, for money. I felt so sorry for one such group that I bought them a meal off a food cart on the side of the road. After that I was their friend as every morning they were waiting for me and would trail behind me on my daily walk around the city. At times I felt like the Pied Piper as I was unable to lose them but I did actually become quite fond of them as these dirty little urchins followed me everywhere. Many times I'd think of my privileged life in England and even my comfortable working life with the Prudential as these street kids were born into a vastly different and ghastly world to mine with not one of them over eight years of age and probably abandoned by their parents. Nearly 100,000 babies are born every day in India and only 40% of all its children go to school as many are born into an impoverished society and who die in shocking numbers where diseases like cholera, tuberculosis and diphtheria are rampant.

On arriving home I couldn't settle down with any normal form of life, especially as an insurance man, as I began to question the poverty that I'd seen and the unfairness there is in the world. Why was it that I had seemingly everything I could have wished for yet nearly a third of the world's people live a grotesque life. On cold winter evenings in my motor car working for the Pru I felt the presence of those street kids all around me. But it was Christmas Day which was to haunt me as I ate my turkey leg I thought of those children I'd befriended and what they would be doing. I didn't need to ask myself that as they would be begging on the streets of Calcutta and in all probability wouldn't even know it was Christmas Day.

# THREE PRU CHARACTERS

There was something quite extraordinary about three characters who worked for The Prudential over many years because the combined total of the three came to 140 years. They really were characters and looking back I think I was most fortunate to have known them as these three insurance men were a law unto themselves. They had a deep suspicion of anyone in authority. This probably happened in view of the sheer number of years they had been employed by the Pru as they may well have thought they were entitled to behave the way they did. I certainly think you couldn't possibly find three such characters in the workplace today, for the simple reason they just don't make them like that anymore.

Sid Bradshaw was one of the old school who undoubtedly did things his own way and in my first couple of years with the Pru, I would frequently knock on his door for advice. Being together in the Stamford district I assumed with all his experience he was the ideal person for me to see, or so I thought. When my section manager would be working elsewhere, I would call at Sid's home with hands full of correspondence which had to be answered amongst many official letters from Prudential offices at Lincoln, Nottingham and Reading. This man, with all his vast experience, then proceeded to tear up the majority of what I thought were important letters and bin them, informing me that I shouldn't worry about such rubbish.

When collecting premiums on his agency he would call at a certain pub, not to buy a drink but to eat his home-made sandwiches and drink from his flask of tea. Although Sid had business with the landlord, it would infuriate the landlord that Sid would never buy a drink. On eating his sandwiches, Sid would then hold court with the locals on the main subject of all his conversation, being Peterborough United (The Posh). He was really passionate in his support for The Posh as such talk would dominate everything else and he wasn't afraid to express his political views either, being a true blue Conservative. I wondered sometimes what his customers really thought of him and were they prepared to listen to his views as he could be most emphatic on such topics. Once he went with a Prudential colleague and their wives for a holiday in Blackpool. In the hotel where they stayed the names of the Posh and the Conservative Party were regularly mentioned by Sid. He talked about nothing else his Pru colleague told me, much to the sadness of other holiday makers.

One day Sid was programmed with the life inspector and in one house the canvass had gone well. The life inspector had asked the man concerned to sign the proposal form but at that precise moment of the completion of the sale, Sid asked the man if he had seen the Posh play lately. This remark completely ruined a brilliant canvass by the life inspector as all talk turned to The Posh. Consequently the man had a change of heart and never did sign the proposal form, much to the obvious annoyance of the life inspector. Dear old Sid always meant well but sometimes would put his foot in it. In his retirement he lived to the age of 80 and when his wife Dorothy died a few years before, Sid cut a very lonely figure. Occasionally I would call to see him and one morning I called he wasn't at all well and died later that day.

Tony Dunn I had heard of before I actually met him as his reputation had gone before him. I only got to know him when the Stamford district office was closed and I was transferred to the Spalding district. What a character he was and one couldn't fail to like him and the stories about him on his agency were legendary. He was another who had to do things his way and wouldn't change for anyone. He could reel off all the funny jokes while smoking his cigarettes and supping whisky in his favourite pub. He worked for the Pru nearly 50 years and actually started as an apprentice. Having done his bit in the armed forces during the war, he returned to the Pru where he continued to be for the rest of his working life. Being an insurance agent, not too many people would have worked for the Pru his amount of time. His agency was in Crowland where he seemed to know everyone and was so well liked by all who came into contact with him.

My own memory of Tony was that he was always falling asleep at district meetings where it seemed literally impossible for him to stay awake. I am sure it didn't bother him much whatever people thought of him if he was asleep or not. It really amazed me at the Spalding district meetings that over the years the district manager allowed him to doze off whilst the rest of the staff would be required to concentrate on what we were being told. I shall always remember when about 30 members of the Spalding district were required to visit the headquarters of the industrial branch of The Prudential at Reading which employed over 3,000 people there. We must have visited a good 12 different departments and everywhere we were taken, on sitting down Tony would fall asleep and not a word was said to him. I did wonder how he managed to drive his car on his agency without falling asleep. Recently his wife Olga told me that after collecting the I.B. premiums from the vicarage at Crowland, he would inform the Vicar at Crowland Abbey that he was going into the church for a sleep, which was a regular occurrence for him. Olga also told me when they were courting, instead of holding hands in the pictures like courting couples did, Tony would instead fall asleep missing the whole film. To have known Tony Dunn was an experience in itself, if only to see him fast asleep without a care in the world.

Dick Megginson - they broke the mould when this character came along as he was one out of the ordinary. If Tony Dunn was known for his sleeping, then chirpy little Dick Megginson was known for talking. He would talk a donkey's hind leg off as I am sure his customers would testify too. I have to say, however, if I was fighting in the trenches in war time would want this man beside me as he would give his absolute all and more. I know he could be an annoying little devil at times and he was capable of having an argument with anyone just to prove he was right, but often it was done in a mischievous sort of way and sometimes he would be quite funny with a twinkle in his eye having proved his point. The more I got to know him the more friendly we became. That wasn't always the case because during the years I was in the Stamford district we would have inter-district cricket matches against the Spalding district. These cricket matches would be the first time I had ever seen him, or should I say it was the first time I heard him as his mutterings on the field of play could be heard everywhere and his attitude could be upsetting to the opposition. I know we in the Stamford district thought he was too cocky for his own good so years later when I joined the Spalding district I was well aware of Dick Megginson but I quickly realised, however, what a lovable character he was.

(a)     At the Spalding staff union meetings I soon discovered that Dick was in his element and could be quite militant at times. Shades of Arthur Scargill, I thought.

(b)     When the deputy lady collector collected premiums on Dick's agency while he was on  holiday, she  learned from his customers that because of his constant chatter he'd still be collecting premiums at 10 o'clock at night.

(c)    The training instructor at a training meeting informed those who attended that he didn't want anyone to smoke (this was before any smoking ban came into existence). Dick then proceeded to light a cigarette informing the instructor he had no right whatsoever to try to stop him smoking.

(d)    When Dick was not on his agency he could often be found in the Spalding district office speaking to the District Manager about goodness knows what. This so infuriated the District Manager that when he knew Dick was in the building he'd lock his office door in order to keep him out.

(e)    Years ago when Dick was a young man, the divisional manager interviewed him. When he heard that Dick was a semi-professional footballer with Spalding United where he was being paid a small weekly wage, the divisional manager told Dick that he must put his job as an insurance agent first. Dick informed him that providing he didn't neglect his work, neither him nor anyone else could stop him playing football.

All the three characters mentioned are now dead. They certainly left their mark with me so where would we find such characters today? I am afraid that in the society we have now they no longer exist and for me I believe communities and the workplace are poorer for that.

# COMPUTER COLLECTING BOOKS

My last 5 years with The Prudential were all change and the older I got I deeply resented such change. One of those changes was the introduction of the new computer collecting book which was to replace the agent's hand-written collecting book. I lived in fear of this new machine and it worried me considerably as to whether I would be able to grasp the workings of it. This computer collecting book was small enough to carry on one's person and had all the information possible as regards names and addresses of all my I.B. customers, along with all the weekly and monthly premiums I was to collect on my agency. All I had to do was to press the appropriate button and all would be revealed on the computer screen. What could be simpler I was told as I attended a two-day training course for all the company's agents in the Spalding district. I was given a large instruction book to study but in the early days this new collecting book could be temperamental and sometimes, on pressing the wrong button, the machine was damaged beyond repair.

I must admit I never thought I'd learn the workings of this new machine and the big instruction book frightened me to death. Because of my ignorance I had already broken two machines. Three times a dispatch rider arrived at my house on his motor bike from chief office with a new machine. Then some admin supervisor arrived from Nottingham asking me what the problem was and then said "do you know that each new computer collecting book costs The Prudential over twelve hundred pounds each"? I did give my apologies that I had ruined two machines and that I was finding this new style collecting book difficult after all the years of using the old collecting book. It was then he started being quite aggressive and why couldn't I use this machine properly. I then mentioned that I would like to throw it into the River Welland close by and hinted to him that he might follow it. Now I have to say I have lived in my house 35 years and have had hundreds of callers but no-one has left my property quicker as he jumped into his car and sped down the road.

The end of this story is most gratifying in that I did eventually learn to work this computer machine and admit that it really was a much easier way of collecting premiums. So when I arrived home after a big collecting day I would press a button and on the screen would be the day's takings. Now that's what I call progress.

# THE WAY WE WERE

It is an undeniable fact that the general public in Great Britain today do not have the amount of life assurance they once had on their lives. This has happened with the demise of the home service insurance man and I believe the country is poorer for that for the simple reason that the old style insurance man is now in permanent decline and virtually lost to all the households he would call upon. Consequently millions of people all over Great Britain now have literally no life assurance in comparison to what they would have had just 20 years ago. The home service insurance man did such a worthwhile and, indeed, valuable job for all his policyholders he would call upon that when one takes The Prudential as an example which when in its prime had business in one in every five homes throughout the country, one is therefore talking about millions of homes. Not forgetting also the other home service insurance companies which were operating exactly like The Prudential and combining all those companies together the amount of people who had life assurance in the event of their death would be astronomical. This indeed was the way we were.

I cannot emphasise enough the significance over the loss of the old style home service insurance man who would be seen out on his agency collecting premiums and searching for new business. That situation has now subsequently disappeared which has ultimately left a heavy strain on Government resources because now in the event of a person's death there may be no life assurance on the deceased. So if the family have no finances whatsoever, the state it seems will pay for the funeral. This is indeed a sorry state of affairs where previously in my 30 years with The Prudential people had a certain pride and responsibility by having their own life assurance policy. Not so any more with the loss of the insurance man but the attitude these days seems to be that a minority of people do not seem to bother about their own life assurance cover. Whatever happened to the independent type of person who would not be reliant on receiving any financial support from anyone? The older they became, my customers were more self-reliant over such things and insisted they have their own life assurance policy in the event of their death and wouldn't be a burden to anyone as regards payment of their own funeral expenses.

# YESTERDAY ONCE MORE

Having a week's holiday at home decorating and being interrupted by customers who called to see me. Often it would be a claim of some sort or a cover note required having changed their motor car. A holiday at home could be a calamity as half the week I could be working for the Pru and if I didn't get away this was a regular occurrence. I always came to the conclusion, however, that working from home was very much part and parcel of an insurance man's occupation and I always accepted it as such.

On completing a death claim form for an elderly lady she was so upset and in tears that both her only daughter and only grandson had been killed in a dreadful road accident. By the time I left her I was nearly in tears myself and the poor lady died of a broken heart months later.

A man aged 83 and a widower spent two and a half days in his bath having been unable to get out. His neighbour, concerned that he hadn't seen him, thought he heard a cry from his neighbour's bathroom window. He then quickly broke into the house and lifted the man out of the bath. "I thought I was going to die there" the insured later informed me.

I'd finally convinced a woman of the importance of having a house contents policy in her house. As she had no cover whatsoever in the event of there being a fire claim. Within a month of the policy being issued a fire started in her kitchen which rapidly gutted the whole of the ground floor. The Prudential met the claim in full, much to the woman's obvious delight.

A divorced woman permitted her two dogs to sleep on her bed but in winter she allowed the dogs to sleep between the sheets with her. "They keep me warm" she said.

A woman customer told me over a cup of tea that her husband had gone off sex with her. With both being in their middle fifties and looking straight at me said "I'm worried that I might start to fancy a younger man the older I get". I would be about 35 years of age at that particular time and on hearing such talk I scarpered out of that house as fast as my little legs would carry me.

Two funerals I got terribly wrong. Turning up at the church I found no-one there and I was told later it was at the crematorium. The other one I turned up at the crematorium only to be told the funeral had taken place the day before. A farmer having been badly burgled started to sleep with a shotgun at the side of his bed, being more prepared for any further burglaries. The insured informed me "If they come again I'll murder them". He would too.

After spending a good hour with a client and having finally persuaded him that being married with young children and a heavy mortgage he should have some life assurance in the event of his death, a week later he had changed his mind. I always found this quite infuriating having done all the hard work only for a person to have a change of heart. This happened occasionally over the years I worked for the Pru and it was always so disappointing but I had to accept that these things do happen as people have every right to change their mind.

Often I'd be required to find prospects for young salesmen who had just been promoted. This worried me as I didn't like the idea that these salesmen might upset my customers with their persistence. Later I'd be told what I feared, that these salesmen had upset my customers who would tell me later "Please do not send any young whippersnapper like you did as I'll only speak to you in future".

An elderly lady whom I knew very well indeed was beaten up by her son in her flat because she refused to give him money to satisfy his drug habit. This shocking incident proved that a drug addict will go to any lengths to get money for drugs.

In my thirty years with The Prudential I was most fortunate in that my health was so good that I never had the need to draw any sickness benefit. I remember once having 'flu and on seeing the doctor he put me off work for a week. Two days later I tore up the doctor's certificate as I felt much better. To be perfectly honest, I couldn't afford to be off work.

Playing local cricket the fast bowler hit me in the groin while batting against him which left me doubled up in pain. He knew I was an insurance man and asked if I was all right when a smile came over his face and he remarked "I presume you are well insured". After the match we had a laugh about the incident and out of curiosity I said to him "I presume you are well insured also". He surprised me by saying he hadn't any life assurance at all but he'd been thinking that he should have some so I made an appointment to see him and I sold him a good sized O.B. policy. Doesn't it show though that once an insurance man, always an insurance man wherever the place may be, in this instance having started on the cricket field.

When I was 18 I went on holiday to Skegness where I met a young teenage boy who was my age and came from Worksop in Nottinghamshire. For a whole week we knocked about together and for a short time kept in touch. The story now moves on an incredible 35 years where I'm at home waiting to greet my new section manager for the first time. A motor car pulls up outside my house and out steps a familiar face but I couldn't put a name to it although I was convinced I had met him before. Even when he told me his name was David

Vaughan it still didn't register with me. But after a couple of weeks it came to me and he was the teenager who I'd palled up with all those years ago at Skegness. David was as amazed as I was that we should meet up again and my only regret was that he was working in the Spalding District for only a short time. It really was good to make his acquaintance once more which proves how small the world can be at times.

I had a customer who over the years had quite a lot of G.B. insurance with me but he just happened to be the most irresponsible and unreliable person one could meet. The excessive worry he gave me made me wonder many a time why I should bother with all the hassle he would give me. Whenever he wrote a cheque, I would worry whether it would bounce or not. By far the biggest worry was when he changed his motor car and would forget to contact me that he wanted a cover note. Fortunately, after a day or two, he realised he'd got to contact me and to my enormous relief he hadn't had a motor accident during this period. He really was the most disorganised businessman I'd ever met and it's a wonder he didn't lose his business before he did. It was virtually impossible to make an appointment to see him as often he'd be travelling around the country. His business deteriorated alarmingly at the finish but, unfortunately, he only had himself to blame. The business he was in was one of the first and if he had been successful he might have made a fortune.

A neighbour woman friend was going shopping in Peterborough and I'd asked her if she would call at the Prudential office in the city and collect my Psion machine, having left it in the office the previous week. This small machine not much bigger than a mobile phone was used by all the company's selling staff to work out premiums etc. The correct pronunciation however of this word Psion can be difficult to pronounce for some people and this dear woman proved to be one such person, so on entering this Prudential office she found it full of people and because of the constant noise being made, the woman proceeded to raise her voice significantly enough to be heard and said rather loudly in the reception area "I've come to collect Mr. Holdich's Psion machine". Now there is another way of pronouncing the name Psion which this woman undoubtedly said and it brought an entirely different interpretation of the word. Evidently the people in that office couldn't believe their ears and roared with laughter which for anyone with a broad imagination would give them much to speculate about. "I've never felt so embarrassed in all my life" the woman meekly told me and I could only apologise for the unfortunate position she had found herself in.

# REDUNDANCIES

It was in 1991 that the Spalding District of the Prudential ceased to exist, with virtually all the District's field staff being transferred to the Peterborough District, which included me. I'm sure that everyone who was employed by the Pru realised that changes were imminent, and we knew that hundreds of district offices all over the country would face closure.

So in September 1992, I, along with thousands of other field staff members throughout the UK, was made redundant at the age of 58. I considered myself one of the lucky ones in view of my age and the years employed by the Pru, I qualified for a good pension and redundancy package. I had got a very good deal but some of my work colleagues in their thirties and forties were not as fortunate as they had to find employment elsewhere. So with the company making thousands redundant, the field staff left were a shadow of its former self.

The main reason for these redundancies had evidently happened because the I.B. collections paid weekly or monthly were disappearing fast and the increased popularity of bank accounts with the growth of direct debits in the ordinary branch meant that O.B. policies were giving better value. The I.B. policies were generally felt to offer poor value and perhaps old-fashioned with premiums still being collected at the door and the time of growing consumer choice, this made the I.B. difficult to promote any more. It meant that the central aims of re-organising the company's sales operation was to accelerate the move to direct debit. So within about a few years from when I had been made redundant all collections made in the I.B. branch had virtually gone. I suppose it was inevitable that one day I.B. collections would cease to exist.

The day I was made redundant I joined an old Prudential friend, David Horner, for a game of snooker at the Peterborough Conservative Club. For once it didn't matter who won the snooker as we had other things to talk about and over a couple of pints of beer we contemplated out future, in other words life after the Pru. Although I had always had many outside interests away from work over the years, I did wonder on that particular day what the future would hold for me. I remember saying that if I was given another 10 years to live I'd be eternally grateful and David said something similar. Above all else, we would hopefully enjoy good health in our retirement. Eighteen years later we are still very much here and still meet occasionally for a game of snooker. When we meet the name Prudential is regularly mentioned and how grateful we are for that Pru pension.

# AN EXCITING LIFE

As I've already written in this book, I had a rather unstable period in my early twenties as I became desperate to find a more settled occupation. I believe that just occasionally in life one may be fortunate enough to have that stroke of luck that can definitely prove to be a life changing experience. It was only because my wife saw an advertisement in the local paper that an insurance agent was required that I was able to join The Prudential, which undoubtedly changed my life. A further piece of good fortune was that my section manager was Bob Sergeant who at times was extraordinarily patient with me. Where perhaps a different personality would not have tolerated me as I really did struggle to come to terms with all the bookwork I was required to do, eventually I overcame adversity and made the grade.

I felt I was in my pomp being an insurance agent and well suited for the job, primarily because I enjoyed meeting people and not only writing up new business with them, but showing genuine interest in them and their families. I'm not saying for one moment I was a roaring success or a glorious failure as it is not for me to speculate as others would judge me on that, but if I could be judged on the service I gave to my customers then hopefully they would say I was always there for them when they wanted me. On reflection I treasure the good times and lasting friendships made above everything else. As regards the bad times, I have conveniently erased them from my memory even though I've written about them. It is, of course, the good times I shall always cherish working for the Pru which brought me contentment and, indeed, security having lived to the age I am so I can really enjoy my Prudential pension.

On being made redundant I had a couple of opportunities to stay in the insurance world as a colleague with the Pru was also made redundant and had opened his own insurance shop and wanted me to join him. Also I'd had a very pressing invitation to work for an insurance broker from Leicester who was keen to expand his business in the Market Deeping area hoping I might persuade my old customers to leave the Pru in order to sell his policies. I have to say I never seriously considered either of these two offers. How could I sell another company's policies after all the years employed by The Prudential? I was about to start drawing my Pru pension so my answer was an emphatic No. Surely the very principles of loyalty were involved here as I wasn't prepared to knock out Prudential policies that I may have originally sold. I know that if I had been made redundant ten years previously, the situation would have been entirely different as I would literally have had to find further employment somewhere else, preferably in the insurance industry, but fortunately I was never put in that predicament.

Ever since I finished work now eighteen years ago, I've lived a very busy and active life and involved in many different activities. It was soon after being made redundant that I was approached by various groups of people asking if I would give a lecture on my experiences in the sub-continent of India. Over the years I have really enjoyed giving these lectures which I have now extended to speak on other subjects. My very latest speaking engagement is about this very subject I am writing about "The Man from The Pru". My attitude is that if I can get the audience laughing by bringing in humorous incidents of my days as an insurance man then I know I am winning them over as my enthusiasm for the subject is plain to see. So if I can bring a smile to a person's face either by hearing me speak or reading this book, then I shall be well pleased. Recently a woman on hearing me speak about "The Man from The Pru" said to me afterwards "What an exciting life you must have had on working for the Pru". So as I finish this book, how can I possibly improve on such a remark and I will happily leave it at that.